BLACKWORK EMBROIDERY

A portrait of Mary Cornwallis ascribed to George Gower, and probably painted *circa* 1590. She is seen wearing a cartwheel ruff, blackwork-embroidered sleeves with gauze oversleeves, and a forepart, or decorative panel filling in the open front of her gown, embroidered in a strapwork pattern.

(Courtesy of the City Art Gallery, Manchester)

Elisabeth Geddes and Moyra McNeill

BLACKWORK EMBROIDERY

DOVER PUBLICATIONS, INC., NEW YORK

International Standard Book Number: 0-486-23245-X
Library of Congress Catalog Card Number: 75-31285

Manufactured in the United States of America
Dover Publications, Inc.
180 Varick Street
New York, N.Y. 10014

Contents

Publisher's Note

MANY of the materials listed in section five are no longer available, and some of the suppliers are no longer in business. Readers are urged first to contact their local art needlework shop or department. Many shops now stock even-weave fabrics and special threads and needles. If you have trouble locating materials, the following wholesale suppliers will be glad to refer you to specific retail outlets.

American Crewel and Canvas Studio
P. O. Box 298
Boonton, New Jersey 07005

Brunswick Worsted Mills, Inc.
230 Fifth Avenue
New York, New York 10001

Kreinik Mfg. Company
1351 Market Street
Parkersburg, West Virginia 26101

Ginnie Thompson Originals, Inc.
P. O. Box 825
Pawleys Island, South Carolina 29585

Joan Toggitt, Ltd.
1170 Broadway
New York, New York 10001

Bernhard Ulmann
230 Fifth Avenue
New York, New York 10001

United Stamped Linen
319 Grand Street
New York, New York 10002

Acknowledgments

THANKS are due to the National Portrait Gallery, London, for permission to reproduce the portraits of Sir Christopher Hatton and Catherine Howard, and to the Kunsthistorisches Museum, Vienna, for supplying a photograph of the portrait of Jane Seymour from which the sleeve detail has been reproduced. Also to The City Art Gallery, Manchester, for permission to reproduce the painting of Mary Cornwallis. The Victoria and Albert Museum and Library, and the British Museum Library, for much invaluable reference material. Messrs. Chapman & Hall, Ltd for permission to quote in the Introduction an extract from *The Craftsman's Plant Book* by Richard Hatton. Messrs. Bernard Quaritch, Ltd and University College, London, for permitting the use of various figures from *Decorative Patterns from the Ancient World* by Sir Flinders Petrie on pages 21 to 23. Messrs. Penguin Books, Ltd for permission to quote some lines from the Penguin *Canterbury Tales* translated by Nevill Coghill.

Thanks also to the following for kindly allowing the reproduction of their privately owned works. Group-Captain Loel Guinness, O.B.E., for permission to reproduce the portrait of *Captain Thomas Lee* on loan to the Tate Gallery (who kindly provided the print). The Governors of St Olave's Grammar School, S.E.1, for permission to reproduce the *Portrait of an Unknown Lady*. The Head of School, Gray's School of Art, Aberdeen, for permitting the inclusion of a photograph of the Dorothy Haegar panel from the school's permanent collection.

Grateful acknowledgments, too, to the various individuals and firms who have generously supplied information, or practical help, or both. They include *Ambassador* magazine; Mr E. A. Entwisle of Wall Paper Manufacturers, Ltd; Dr Strong of the National Portrait Gallery; Mr R. C. Carrington, Headmaster of St Olave's Grammar School; Mr P. du Sautoy and Messrs. Faber & Faber, Ltd; Mr John Pinder-Wilson; The Embroiderers' Guild; Mr H. Phelps of the Wray Park Studio, Reigate; Mr Brian McNeill; Mr J. R. Pilcher; and embroidery students at Hammersmith College of Art and Building.

Finally, but not least in importance, we must thank our Editor and Publishers for their monumental patience during the preparation of this book.

Introduction

RECENTLY there has been a revival of interest in blackwork and its possibilities in modern embroidery. Unlike so many of our traditional methods, this type of black on white needlework, if approached in a twentieth-century manner, can be given a most satisfyingly crisp and up-to-date look. Historically, blackwork was first and foremost associated with dress, and its study is necessarily linked with the study of sixteenth- and early seventeenth-century costume styles, where alterations in fashion played an important part in influencing its development, although this, of course, was also affected by the trend in Elizabethan domestic embroidery which occurred within the same period.

It is really only possible to appreciate blackwork properly in conjunction with the social and domestic scene in which it flourished. Consequently, the first part of this book consists of a brief historical survey, "for the most part gathered out of sundrie writers" to whom grateful acknowledgment is due, and this attempts to present blackwork not merely as a charming Olde Worlde survival, but as the product of a most interesting way of life and environment which it helps to reflect. Many of the motifs and pattern arrangements used in blackwork and other Tudor embroidery were not restricted to needlework, but were also commonly employed in interior and exterior architectural decoration, such as plaster ceilings, wall-paintings, wood- and stone-carvings and so on, producing a certain unity among all the decorative arts, and giving the period its especial flavour. Numbers of surviving Elizabethan timber-framed houses can be seen today, particularly in Cheshire, Lancashire, and Lincolnshire, which feature in their structural members the same style of bold black-and-white patterning found in blackwork.

Embroidery in the Tudor and early Stuart periods was an inseparable part of the routine of everyday life for the upper and middle classes. To try to imitate it today is wrong, simply because it expresses a society quite different from ours in its surroundings and ways of thought. Hence the second part of the book tries to show some of the decorative possibilities blackwork can have *today*, suited to a twentieth-century setting, with modern materials and threads, and with an inevitably different function. The designs and interpretations are inevitably limited in scope, but what matters is for the designer to realise that in embroidery, as in all art, the last word can never be said. For those sufficiently interested, there exist opportunities for still further experiment, especially in the use of blackwork for abstract design and collage. As Richard Hatton observes in *The Craftsman's Plant Book*: "To reject skilful methods, to neglect tradition, is not necessarily to be either less civilised, less thoughtful, or less devoted to art. . . ."

A late sixteenth- early seventeenth-century Chalice Veil embroidered in red silk, with a border representing symbols of the Passion. Diaper fillings, with plaited braid and outline stitches.

(Courtesy of the Victoria & Albert Museum. Crown copyright)

One

HISTORICAL SURVEY

"Tell me Dorinda, why so gay?
Why such embroidery, fringe, and lace?
Can any dresses find a way
To stop the approaches of decay,
And mend a ruin'd face?"

Lord Dorset

BLACKWORK, as an embroidery method, must be so well known as to require only the briefest definition. In its widest sense, it is the embroidery in black silk on white linen which became fashionable during the reign of Henry VIII, continuing in use throughout the sixteenth century, and dying out some time between 1600 and 1630. In its initial phase, it was known as "Spanish work", and for the first fifty years of its popularity seems to have been used principally for dress embroidery. During the reign of Elizabeth I, black-work was utilised for different styles of design, which produced variations in working technique within the method. In this half of the century its scope as a method of decoration increased, and it was worked not only on dress and dress accessories, but on a variety of household articles such as bed-hangings, and other soft furnishings not strictly in general use before the Elizabethan period.

Katharine of Aragon is reputed to have been responsible for introducing blackwork into this country as an innovation from Spain, when she came over in 1501 to marry Arthur Tudor, but there can be little doubt that counted-thread embroidery in black-and-white was known in England well before this. In their book *Needlework through the Ages*, Symonds and Preece remark: ". . . The Spanish people . . . also had the Moorish tradition of white linen embroidered in black, which either in wool or silk they sometimes enriched with metal threads. When Katharine of Aragon came to England . . . she encouraged the Spanish style of embroidery, which in an increasingly rich form became a marked characteristic of Tudor England, but the black embroidery of Katharine was probably not altogether unknown in England before her day. . . ."

13

Embroidery has its roots in many countries and cultures, and it is often impossible to pinpoint the actual source of a particular technique, because research will reveal origins too .ancient and diffuse to be confined within a definite place or period. Types of counted-thread embroidery in black on white are found in many countries, especially the Slavonic countries of Eastern Europe, i.e. Russia, Roumania, Czechoslovakia, Bulgaria, and Yugoslavia, where it has been a peasant industry for centuries. Indisputably the Spanish style introduced by Katharine must have been responsible for *encouraging*, to a greater degree, the fashion for this kind of embroidery among the upper classes, but not necessarily for *starting* it, and this Spanish style during its evolution must have been influenced by traditional methods introduced from North Africa.

Moorish rule in Spain was not finally overthrown until 1492, after a period of nearly eight centuries, during which time Spanish culture had been developed and influenced by her Mohammedan invaders. Spanish decorative art over this period can be seen to express the Islamic principle of symmetry, and the use of geometric motifs and all-over patterning in preference to natural forms. The Moorish era actually resulted in considerable achievements in the textile crafts of Spain, especially silk-weaving, for which she was famous, and also carpet-making and embroidery. Typical Spanish textile patterns in the fifteenth century are based on the lotus and palmette and their derivative forms, a limited number of animal subjects, such as heraldic griffins, lions, and peacocks; also foliate forms—grapevines and leaves, acanthus and rosette forms, and innumerable geometric figures—stars, circles, interlacing quatrefoils, lozenges, rectangles, arabesques. The device of the pomegranate, which is so often associated with Katharine as Queen, came from Granada, the city where she spent her childhood.

By the opening of the sixteenth century, a European era was beginning to dawn in Spain, helped by the spread of fresh artistic and intellectual ideas liberated by the Renaissance, so that by the end of the century Spanish fabrics were no longer ornamented with intricate all-over patterning, but with large individual motifs, as Gothic and Renaissance styles supplanted the geometric Islamic ones. However, at the time of Katharine's arrival in England, the artistic climate of Spain was still essentially Mohammedan, and it is possible to detect in early Tudor blackwork embroidery, where represented in paintings, the type of geometric designs which were then very characteristic of her native country.

Examples of Moorish interlacing patterns from the Alhambra, Granada. 13th to 14th centuries.

The vogue prevalent at this time for embroidering visible portions of the underlinen seems to have begun during the late Middle Ages. The shirt was then the innermost garment worn by both sexes of the wealthier classes, the feminine version being called a smock (Anglo-Saxon) or chemise (Norman). Both shirts and smocks (or chemises) were sometimes made of silk, but more generally of linen, and from the late thirteenth century up to the seventeenth, it was the practice to embroider them at neck and wrists with gold or coloured silk. There must be few who are not familiar with a certain passage in the *Canterbury Tales,* where Chaucer describes Alison the carpenter's wife. He says:

> "Her smock was white; embroidery repeated
> Its pattern on the collar front and back,
> Inside and out; it was of silk and black.
> And all the ribbons of her milky mutch
> Were made to match her collar, even such. . . ."[1]

Chaucer's *Tales* were written between 1388 and 1400, so the black embroidery he mentions was a precursor of Tudor work, though most likely dissimilar in appearance. (A mutch was the linen or muslin cap worn by women of that period.)

In the 1480's, at the close of Edward IV's reign, there began the practice of "slashing" or slitting the outer garments, a fashion which continued on into the sixteenth century, when it reached its most exaggerated form. At first slashing was applied to the elbows only, to allow for easier movement, and this led to portions of the inner shirt sleeve being pulled through the slits and displayed for decorative effect. Subsequently, embroidery was added to the exposed portions, and the shirt developed into an important feature of the dress. Planché says: "the opening of the sleeve at the elbow . . . led to another curious fancy, the complete division of the sleeve into two or more pieces, and their attachment to each other by means of points or laces through which the shirt or chemise protruded, for the fashion was not confined to the male sex. . . ."[2]

In the sixteenth century the material used for these undergarments continued to be linen, and for those who could afford the luxury of sheets, towels, and napery, they too were of linen, so also were wall-hangings, either painted or embroidered. An astonishing amount was used, and although much was home-produced, it was necessary to import large quantities from abroad, especially certain of the finer qualities in demand by the wealthy, such as "holland" cloth, and cambric and lawn from Cambrai and Laon in France. In Henry VIII's reign linen cloth imports affected home production to such an extent that an early statute for the encouragement of linen manufacture to ease unemployment, required "every person occupying land for tillage, shall for every sixty acres which he hath under the plough, sow one quarter of an acre in flax or hemp". The technique of weaving cotton from imported spun fibre had reached England during the Crusades, late in the twelfth century, but cotton was slow to find favour as a clothing material in competition with wool and linen, and for some time was more often used mixed with the latter (cotton weft, linen warp) to make a type of cloth called fustian, which was worn by the poorer classes, and sometimes employed for bedding. The defeat of the Spanish Armada in 1588 made it possible to establish the British East India Trading Company at the end of the century, through which England received its first important supplies of raw cotton, and ultimately the importation of Indian cotton muslins displaced the flaxen linens and cambrics in the fashionable world.

[1] Modern translation by Nevill Coghill in the Penguin *Chaucer* 1951.
[2] Planché, *Cyclopaedia of Costume,* vol. II.

Detail from the Holbein portrait of Jane Seymour in the Kunsthistorisches Museum, Vienna, painted in 1536. It shows her slashed undersleeves, the openings thus made drawn together by means of jewelled buttons, and full chemise sleeves pulled through the intervening gaps. The chemise sleeves are finished with cuff ruffles decorated with a wide band of geometric black embroidery.

Throughout the first half of the sixteenth century in England, the dress of the female aristocracy was rigidly confining (as indeed it was also in the second half), simple in its outlines like that of the middle classes, and principally distinguished from the latter by the lavishness of its goldsmith's work and embroidery. Male dress, designed to create an impression of burly and aggressive masculinity, was by contrast more elaborate and exaggerated. It was composed of many different layers of garments, causing a nobleman of the period to complain that men had so many pleats upon their breasts and such puffed sleeves, that it was impossible for them to draw a bow in their coats. For greater comfort, as well as in order to show them off, it was fashionable to wear the various layers open in front. The shirt now became an article of elegant attire, and those worn by the aristocracy were extremely finely woven and very costly. Occasionally they were so fine as to be semi-transparent. Giustiniani, the Venetian Ambassador, impressed by Henry VIII's skill on the tennis-courts, wrote in 1515: ". . . it was the prettiest thing in the world to see him play, his fair skin glowing through a shirt of the finest texture. . . ."

In the Tudor period, clothes and houses provided almost the only outlets for expenditure and display. Embroidery and costly attire were upper-class prerogatives, and the various Sumptuary Laws enacted in Henry's reign, and re-enacted in Elizabeth's, are the best evidence for the differences in dress which were supposed to distinguish various ranks of society. In 1553 an Act of Parliament was passed forbidding every person below the dignity of knight to wear "pinched" (pleated) shirts, or "plain shirtes garnished with silk gold, or silver". In an age when aristocratic fashions customarily took their trend from the personal tastes of the reigning monarch, Henry's interest in the affairs of his fellow sovereigns on the continent resulted in the appearance of a succession of French and Italian fashions at Court. Spanish dress, it seems, did not entirely find favour, except for the adoption of the farthingale. The dark colours, especially black, which Katharine preferred, were considered too gloomy and austere for court taste, but the Spanish style of black embroidery was obviously much admired because it was quickly adopted. One of the King's Inventories of Apparel (M. S. Harl, No. 1419) contains entries of "shirtes wrought with black silke" and "shirtes trimmed with black and white silke". Among the New Year gifts presented to Mary I in 1556, were smocks "wrought with black silk, Spanish fashion". According to Mrs Palliser, the wardrobe accounts of Katharine of Aragon herself contain frequent references to "sheets and pillow-beres (covers) wrought with Spanish work of black silk at the edge", and the inventory of Cardinal Wolsey's effects at Hampton Court Palace, which takes up forty folio pages, lists among his personal beds one which, apart from having eight mattresses, each "stuffed with thirteen pounds of carded wool," had four pillow-covers, "two of them seamed with black silk and fleurs-de-lys of gold. . . ."

Dr Willet Cunnington has stated that Spanish work is not the same as "true" blackwork, which he asserts did not appear until later in the century—some time in the 1530's—during the time of Anne Boleyn, or Jane Seymour. However, "true" blackwork must have grown out of Spanish work, though unfortunately little, if any, of this earlier black embroidery has survived, and we have only contemporary painted portraits to provide a visual record of its manner of use, and the way in which, in conjunction with other parts of the dress, it contributed to the total splendid effect. Judging by the evidence presented by all this portraiture, Spanish work when first introduced seems to have been delicate in quality, and confined to edge treatments, but the increasing lavishness of fashionable dress enabled it to develop ultimately into the richer style. Spanish work is first shown on the neck-bands and wrist-bands of shirts and chemises, then, growing more elaborate, on standing and turn-down collars, the fronts, wrists, and sleeve-frills of men's shirts, and the shirt-sleeves themselves, where pulled through the slashed doublet sleeves. Sometimes the whole front of the shirt is embroidered, and the doublet left open to the waist to display it. Women wear blackwork embroidery on chemise fronts and wrist-frills, and another item of costume which is shown decorated with blackwork is the partlet. This was a separate accessory consisting of a buttoned-down covering to the upper part of the chest and shoulders, with a fitted neck, which was at first collarless, but had a stand-up collar added in the 1530's. The partlet was generally left open in front to show the embroidered chemise underneath. The male version, alternatively called a "plackard", was usually very ornamental, viz: "Eight partlets, three garnished with gold, the rest with Spanish work" (Inventory of Lord Monteagle, 1523, P.R.O.).

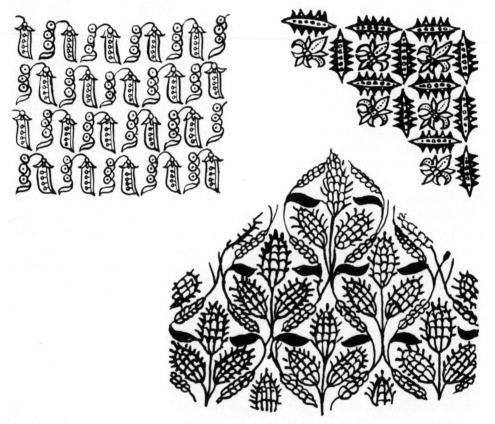

Patterns from Tudor coifs and kerchiefs illustrated in *Needlework as Art* by Lady Alford, published in 1886. They are described as "Henry VIII Spanish work from Louisa, Lady Waterford's collection". Now in the Lord Middleton Collection, on loan to Nottingham Museum.

A portrait of Catherine Howard by Holbein, in the National Portrait Gallery. Her gown sleeves are divided into two separate strips of material, caught together at regular intervals along the upper and lower edges with laces having decorative tags, or aiguillettes; through the gaps are pulled portions of braided undersleeve. Exposed at the wrists are the blackwork cuff ruffles of her chemise. Painted in 1541.

(*Reproduced by courtesy of the National Portrait Gallery, London*)

The art of painting throughout the sixteenth century was principally confined to portraiture, and of those painters who worked in the first half, the most eminent is, of course,
Hans Holbein the Younger, who came to England from Antwerp. His first visit took place
in 1526, at the age of twenty-nine, when he stayed nearly two years; his second was in 1532,
when he settled in England and became court painter to Henry VIII. The various portraits
still existing of Katharine of Aragon and Anne Boleyn are not by him, the first of Henry's
queens he painted being Jane Seymour, and one portrait is now in the Kunsthistorisches
Museum, Vienna. It shows her cuffs decorated with a repeating geometric pattern worked
in a black linear technique. Another portrait, of Catherine Howard, with blackwork wrist
ruffles, is in the Toledo Museum of Art, Ohio, U.S.A. Until his death, about 1543, Holbein
had a greater influence on English art than any of his contemporaries, and there have
survived a large number of paintings by unknown artists which are executed in the Holbein
manner, and have often been wrongly attributed to him. Other painters of note are
Gerlach Flicke, Anthonis Mor, and Guillim Scrots, or Stretes, who worked in England
between 1545 and 1553. The very well-known "Portrait of a Gentleman in Red", at Hampton Court Palace, is attributed to him. It was painted around 1548, and depicts a young
man wearing the voluminous costume of the period, with doublet opened to display the
rich black embroidery of the shirt. With it is another portrait, likewise attributed to
Stretes, of Edward VI, who wears a neck frill embroidered with individual blackwork
motifs, and a third painting, which is of Elizabeth I by an unknown artist, depicts her
wearing blackwork sleeves.

The English were not unique in wearing their linen embellished with black embroidery.
There are portraits by Continental artists at this date, such as the Italian painters Moroni
and Veneto, and some of the Swiss portraits by Holbein, before he settled in England,
which show that this was a widespread European fashion. One result of the Renaissance
had been the emergence of a recognisably international style of costume, brought about by
improved communications, and the growth of foreign travel by scholars and nobles in
pursuit of the New Learning, which brought people of different countries into contact
with each other as never before. Holbein's sitters wear rich black counted-thread embroidery on neck-bands and collars, which resembles Slavonic cross-stitch work, especially
that of Roumania and Bulgaria. In his portrait of Simon George of Quocote (*circa* 1540)
the embroidery appears to be reversible, in which case it might have been carried out in
two-sided cross with double-running. Spanish work is assumed to have been Arabic and
Moorish in origin, but an element of vagueness persists as to the actual techniques of this
African embroidery. Spanish work itself probably employed several different stitches for
its effect—Lady Alford[1] defines it as "white or black silk, and gold lace stitches on fine
linen", and one of these stitches seems to have been used independently as a form of
decoration in its own right, and known as Spanish stitch.

Spanish work could be adapted, apparently, to interpret somewhat different types of
designs, either purely geometric figures forming bands and borders, or formalised patterning based on floral and leaf forms, i.e. acanthus, pomegranate, etc. The embroidery was
sometimes wholly linear, or else dark and toned areas were introduced, especially by tiny

[1] *Needlework as Art*, published 1886.

diaper fillings worked on the thread. These little geometric patterns, which are such a feature of the technique, copy in miniature the Spanish-Moresque motifs used so profusely in the architectural decoration and other applied arts of medieval Spain, but their proto-types can be traced back through early Byzantine to Graeco-Roman and Ancient Greek sources, and well beyond these, to the pattern forms of primitive man. Spanish work was frequently enriched with gold, and occasionally worked entirely in red, characteristics which persisted throughout the century. "Morisco work" was the name given to a type of couched embroidery in gold or silver, using arabesque patterns; "A pair of sleeves of Morisco work" is mentioned in the wardrobe inventory of Henry VIII, 1547.

Ancient textile patterns from plaiting and netting.

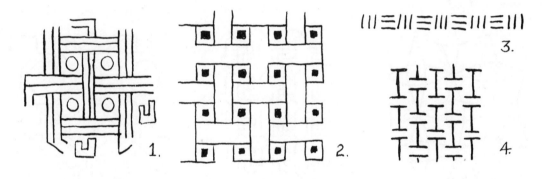

5.

1 From Mochlos.
2 Pompeii.
3 Canosa, N. Apulia. 250 B.C.
4 Athes Maia. Pattern from Gorgon dress, 700 B.C.
5 Pattern from Nimrud saddle-cloth, 730 B.C.

Blackwork Embroidery

Patterns from early pavement mosaics.

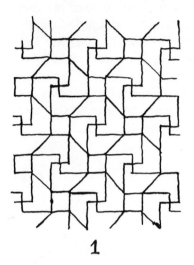

1

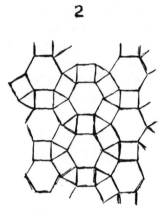

2

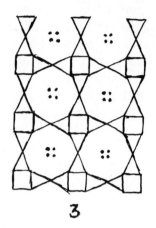

3

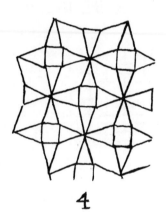

4

5

6

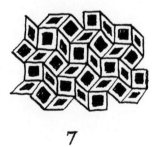

7

8

1, 2, 3, 4 Pompeii, A.D. 60.
5 Pistoia, A.D. 300.
6 Rome, St. Constanza. A.D. 340.
7 Ravenna, A.D. 500.
8 Irish Dysert O'Dea, A.D. 1080.

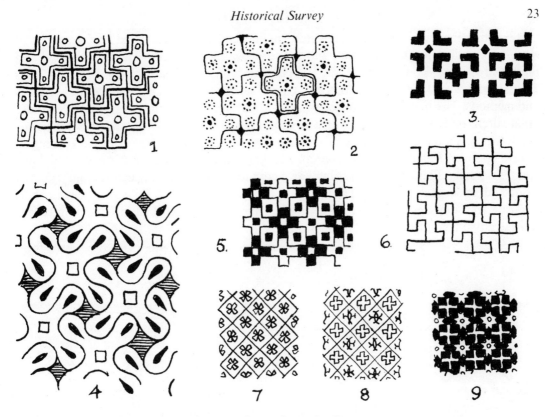

Ancient Pattern forms from the Cross.

1 Mykenae. Pattern from a robe, *circa* 2300 B.C.
2 Knossos, Crete. Pattern on a robe, *circa* 2300 B.C.
3 Novgorod. 1450 B.C.
4 Amenemhat, Egypt. Textile pattern, 1400 B.C.
5 Khorsabad, Assyria, *circa* 1000 B.C.
6 Verruchio. Swastika pattern, 700 B.C.
7, 8 Childeric. Early Christian, A.D. 480.
9 Innsbruck Fibula.

10 Kobour, Osseta, Italy. Key pattern *circa* 680 B.C.
11, 12 Platanos. Decorated squares *circa* 2588 B.C.
13 Hittite.
14 Mohenjo-Daro, early Crete. Division of circle into four when compass-struck patterns were unknown.

Regarding the identity of Spanish stitch, an encyclopedic work called *The Academie of Armory* compiled by the heraldic painter and genealogist, Randle Holme, in 1649, and published in 1688, contains in Book III, chapter 5 under a heading *The School Mistris Terms of Art for All Her Ways of Sowing*, a list of nearly forty different embroidery stitches and methods. The majority are obsolete, and of historic interest only, but the list includes "plat-stitch, or single plat-stitch which is good on one side", "plat-stitch, or double plat-stitch which is alike on both sides", and "Spanish stitch, true on both sides". Turning to today, Thomas' *Dictionary of Stitches* and Dillmont's *Encyclopaedia of Needlework* both give "Two-sided Plaited Spanish stitch" as a counted-thread stitch which is similar on the front and back. According to Thomas it is a border stitch, but Dillmont goes further, and says that any design for cross-stitch embroidery can be worked in it, adding that it has the advantage of being quick to work.

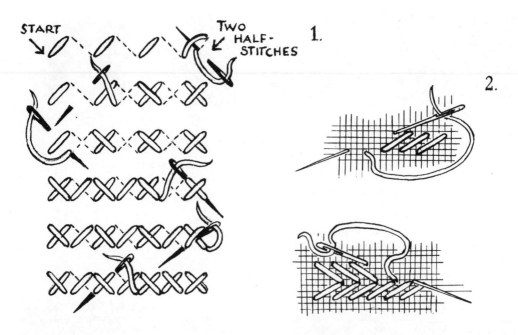

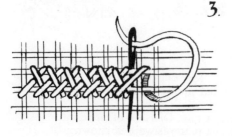

1 Two-sided Cross-stitch worked in four journeys.
From Thomas' Dictionary of Stitches.

2 Two-sided Plaited Spanish stitch.
From the Dillmont Encyclopaedia of Needlework.

3 Plait, or Spanish stitch.
From Thomas' Dictionary of Stitches.

The Thomas *Dictionary*, in addition, gives "Plait stitch, also known as Spanish Stitch", a canvas stitch worked like a less sloped version of Long-Armed Cross, and not identical on both sides. It is not beyond the bounds of possibility that our ancestors' Single Plat has come down to us transferred to canvas, its original link with Spanish work remaining in the name. Or, that their double plat-stitch has become two-sided plaited Spanish stitch, and what today we term double-running was the original Spanish stitch. The embroidery on Jane Seymour's cuffs, in the painting already mentioned (page 16), as well as that represented in many of Holbein's other paintings, is obviously double-running, whereby this stitch has derived its other name of Holbein stitch. Without any actual proof, all this can only be supposition. The only thing of which we can be sure is that it was customary to use reversible stitches on such parts of the dress as the collar and cuffs. Chaucer made this clear when he wrote:

> . . . embroidery repeated
> Its pattern on the collar front and back,
> Inside and out. . . .

It is not surprising that so little embroidery from the first part of the century should have survived, when domestic conditions are taken into account. Professor Brewer describes the early Tudor period as "an age instinct with vast animal life, robust health and muscular energy, terrible in its rude and unrefined appetites, its fiery virtues and fierce passions. . . ." By comparison with the great improvement which took place during Elizabeth's reign, not only appetites, but living conditions as well, were rude and unrefined. Within doors, even in the greatest houses, standards of cleanliness could be very low indeed, if the owner was not sufficiently fastidious—vide Erasmus' celebrated description of the English interior, *circa* 1530: "The floors are commonly of clay strewed with rushes, so renewed that the substratum may lie undisturbed some twenty years. They shelter underneath, spit, vomit, dog and human urine, discarded scraps of venison and fish, and unnameable filth. As a result, in changes of weather, certain vapours are exhaled which, to my way of thinking, are of little benefit to the health of the human body. . . ." It is said that even Wolsey, when crossing his own courtyard, had to hold to his nose ". . . an orange, whereof the meat or substance within was taken out and filled again with a sponge, wherein was vinegar and other confections against the pestilent airs" (Cavendish). Conditions varied, of course, according to personal standards, but damp, dirt, ill-ventilation, and perhaps more important, scarcity of furniture and inadequate provision for storage, must all have combined to produce an unfavourable environment for preserving perishable fabrics. To these must surely be added the adverse effects of smoke, for until the mid-century chimneys were something of a rarity even in the noblest houses, and fires burnt on open hearths, the smoke escaping as best it might through special apertures in the roof. Even though Wolsey built his palace at Hampton Court with many splendid brick chimneys, the Great Hall, a later replacement by Henry VIII, followed the old custom by having its fireplace set in the middle of the floor near the dais, and a louvre high up in the roof to permit rising smoke to escape. Such an arrangement must have made the principal rooms of English houses distinctly smoky in the winter, especially when the wind was in an unfavourable

quarter. As long as wood fires were burnt this could be endured, but coal-smoke, when coal began to replace wood, was found intolerable, a circumstance, among others, which gave impetus to the adoption of chimneys with chimney-flues. Even so, the earlier open fireplace still had its devotees. "Now we have many chimneys," wrote William Harrison, the Elizabethan biographer and antiquary, "and yet our tenderlings complain of rheumes, catarrhs and poses. . . . For as the smoake in those days was supposed to be a sufficient hardening for the timbers of the house, so it was reputed to be a far better medicine to keep the goodman and his family from the quack."

Regarding early storage methods, the Countess of Wilton observes ". . . clothes were not formerly kept in drawers, where but a few can be laid with due regard for the safety of each, but were hung up on wooden pegs in a room appropriated to the sole purpose of receiving them; and though such cast-off things as were composed of rich substances were occasionally ripped for domestic uses, (viz: mantles for infants, vests for children, and counterpanes for beds) articles of inferior quality were suffered to *hang by the walls* till age and moths had destroyed what pride would not permit to be worn by servants or poor relations . . ."[1] and she mentions Shakespeare's allusion to this in *Cymbeline*, where Imogen exclaims:

> "Poor I am stale, a garment out of fashion,
> And, for I am richer than to hang by the walls,
> I must be ripp'd. . . ."

Another destructive factor must have been the crude soap used for laundering. Soap was first home-made in the fourteenth century, mainly for laundry purposes, as toilet-waters of various kinds (also home produced) were employed for a long time for personal use. Laundry soap, according to Harrison in his *Description of England*, published in 1577, was compounded of cow-dung, hemlock, nettles and refuse soap "than which there is none more unkindly savour", while as late as 1700, John Houghton, a Fellow of The Royal Society, wrote: "Formerly bucking[2] with lees made of our English ashes and hog's dung were very much used for the washing of clothes, but for aught I can learn, whenever soap comes, it gets ground of these as being more neat, sweet and less troublesome." The Soapers' or Soapmaker's Company was not incorporated until 1638, when the ingredients were alkali salt obtained from potash, with tallow and olive-oil "intimately mixed by boiling: in help whereof the unctuous parts of the tallow and oil do incorporate with the grease that is on foul linen etc. and the alkali salts do so far divide the greasy particles that they are capable of being diluted which by themselves they would not be. . . ." Houghton also noted that the product was "extraordinary dear"—it was threepence a pound, roughly the equivalent of six shillings today.

[1] *The Art of Needlework*, Countess of Wilton. Published 1840.
[2] Washing or bleaching in lye.

Left
"Portrait of an Unknown Lady" *circa* 1587, attributed to John Bettes. The lady wears a magnificent wired cut-work collar, edged with lace, and sleeves richly embroidered with large blackwork floral motifs beneath gauze oversleeves.
(*Courtesy of the Headmaster and Governors of St Olave's Grammar School, London, S.E.1.*)

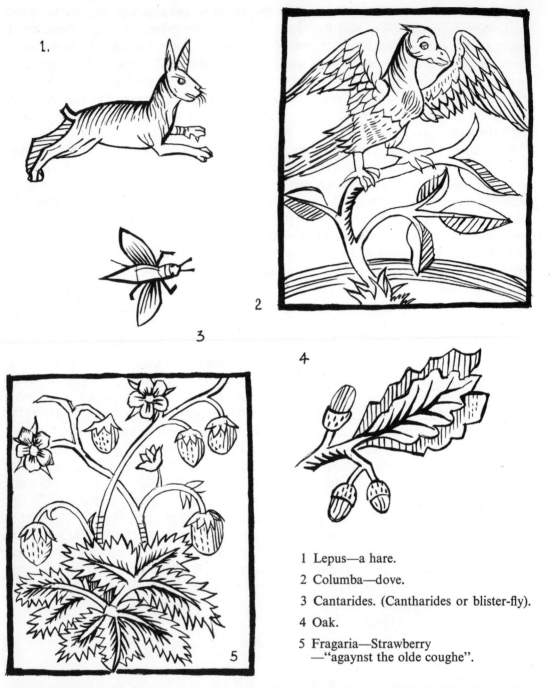

1 Lepus—a hare.

2 Columba—dove.

3 Cantarides. (Cantharides or blister-fly).

4 Oak.

5 Fragaria—Strawberry
—"agaynst the olde coughe".

Woodcut illustrations from the *Grete Herball* of Peter Treveris, printed in Southwark in 1529. It expounds the curative properties of plants, and other forms of wild life, and the good or bad effects derived from eating various kinds of flesh.

(*From the British Museum*)

Historically, the first half of the sixteenth century was a period of transition between the end of the Middle Ages and the beginning of Renaissance England—between the medieval and the modern world. As the century advances, certain Renaissance architectural features appear in the form of superficial additions to the late Gothic style, such as an abundance of imposed ornamental strapwork and scrolling. This type of Renaissance decoration is reflected in Tudor embroidery designs, which passed from the earlier, rather stiff style to a freer, more exuberant Elizabethan interpretation, having a uniquely national form of expression.

A very important factor in the progress of sixteenth-century embroidery was the appearance of pattern-books. By the time of Caxton's death in 1491, various presses had been set up in England, but their standard of printing was poor, and most English books were printed abroad and imported. It was not until Elizabeth came to the throne that the standard of book-production at home made any notable improvement. The earliest pattern-books contained the minimum of text apart from a title-page with description of the book's contents, publisher's puff, and occasionally a dedication. The illustrations were usually wood-cuts, although later in the century they began to be cut in soft metal in the manner of wood-cuts. The blocks themselves not infrequently travelled around perhaps to several countries, re-appearing in quite different books, or else block-makers copied from imported illustrations that took their fancy. As the actual pages of the books had to be pricked during the transferring operation, surviving books are very rare. One of the earlier imports during Henry VIII's reign was William Vorsterman's *A Neawe Treatys as cocernynge the excellency of the Nedleworecke Spanisshe stitche and Weavynge in the frame. . . .* This was published *circa* 1530, by P. Quentel. A little later, in 1548, the first embroidery pattern-book to be printed in England appeared. It was engraved on copper by a surgeon, Thomas Geminus, and entitled *Moryssche & Damaschin renewed & encreased very profitable for Goldsmiths & Embroiderars.* It featured arabesque designs, and only one copy is now in existence.

During Elizabeth's reign the quality of printing and book-production in England considerably improved, and there was an ever-increasing flow of books from English presses, although many English books were still printed abroad. The visual affinity of black on white embroidery with printed illustration, gave rise to the use of motifs and designs which were often copied directly from engravings, not only from pattern-books specially intended for embroidery, but from herbals, bestiaries, and translations from Greek and Latin writings (such as *Æsop's Fables*). The Elizabethans had the benefit of a greater literary output than was available in the earlier half of the century, and there was still a considerable interchange of illustrative matter going on between English and foreign presses. Of the Elizabethan pattern-books, some famous ones which have survived are Geoffrey Whitney's *A Choice of Emblems & other Devises* printed in Leyden and published in 1586 with a dedication to the Earl of Leicester, wherein Whitney describes the book as "gatheringes and gleaninges out of other mens harvestes. . . ." Also John Wolfe's *New & Singular Patternes & Workes on Linnen* published in 1592 from a work by an Italian, F. Vinciola: and in 1596, William Barley's *A Booke of Strange Inuentions called the First Part of Needleworkes . . .* The *Commonplace Book* of Thomas Trevelyan, and *A Scholehouse*

Part of an illustration of "the manured vine" taken from *The Herball or General Historie of Plantes* by John Gerard, published in 1597, and sub-titled "Plantes . . . gathered by John Gerard of London, Master of Chirurgerie."

(*From the British Museum*)

For the Needle by Richard Shorleyker, were both published in the next century, in 1608 and 1624 respectively, but they contain typical Elizabethan motifs.

The printed herbals were first confined to setting out contemporary lore concerning the medicinal and healing properties of plants, but as the cultivation of gardens began to develop into an Elizabethan passion, they were expanded into general botanical studies. *The New Herball* or *Herbal of William Turner* was published in 1568, followed by *A Niewe Herball, or Historie of Plantes* by Henry Lyte in 1578. Gerard's famous *The Herball, or General Historie of Plantes* appeared in 1597.

Sir Christopher Hatton, painted by an unknown artist. His collar and cuffs are shown trimmed with lace, and decorated with blackwork embroidery in a scrolling pattern of pomegranates and flowers.

(*Courtesy of The National Portrait Gallery, London*)

Sixteenth-century bestiaries reflected popular interest in the strange and exotic fauna encountered by English traders and explorers during their excursions into the New World. The bestiaries pictured and described these animals, with others more familiar, and also mythological creatures in great variety. The best known include Conrad Gesner's *Historia Animalium* printed at Zurich and published in 1551, Edward Wooton's *Differentus Animalum* published in 1552, Nicholas de Bruyn's *Animalium Quadrepedum* published in Antwerp in 1594, and Topsell's *Historie of Four-footed Beastes* which appeared in 1606. Embroiderers found such book-illustrations ideal for translating into needlework, and towards the end of the century there begin to appear in blackwork, as also in other forms of embroidery, such non-indigenous creatures as monkeys, elephants, camels, and crocodiles, and, even more popular, fabulous monsters like the unicorn, phoenix, and cockatrice.

Elizabeth's reign brought with it a period of peace, prosperity, and expanding trade for England. The country's wealth became more widely distributed throughout the population instead of being concentrated in a few hands, and this resulted in a general rise in the standard of living and material comfort. Blackwork came into wider use for the decoration of soft furnishings in addition to dress, and it is significant that from this half of the century, when domestic conditions began to show a definite improvement, many specimens of contemporary blackwork have survived. The main impact of the Renaissance in sixteenth-century England is to be found in the flowering of Elizabethan literature and drama, but it was also reflected in the richness and vanity of national dress. Elizabethan upper-class costume is acknowledged to be the most gorgeous and elaborate of all historic styles, and it became more and more lavish as time went on. Again, we are able to turn to the work of contemporary painters, Cornelius Ketel, the younger Gheeraerts, Sir A. Mor, Eworth, George Gower, who painted the portraits of Sir Thomas and Lady Kitson in the Tate Gallery, and the great miniaturist Nicholas Hilliard, for a survey of Elizabethan dress.

Men's shirts were still exquisitely embroidered in gold, coloured silk or blackwork, though less of it was visible owing to the high-necked doublet, except where this was slashed. At the opening of the century, the shirt neck-line had been low, appearing just above the doublet and edged with a band. Later, by 1525, it was being cut higher, though still finished with a band. By 1530, the band had become a standing collar at the neck, edged either with a turn-down collar called a falling-band, or a frill, which developed by stages into the ruff. The ruff was smallish and limp until the 1560's, when starching and goffering were introduced, starch, called by the Puritans "devil's liquor", having been invented in Holland specifically for use with the ruff. The tubular pleats were known as "sets" and were arranged in varying degrees of complexity, from the simple figure-of-eight set in one layer, to compound sets of massed convolutions in several layers. There were variations in size—small, medium, and the cartwheel ruff. As the size of ruffs increased, they became detached from the shirt to form a separate article, and were often worn as well as a falling band. The cartwheel ruff, which came in between 1580 and 1610, was up to 18 inches in diameter, and had to be supported on a wire "underpropper". It was closed all round, and nicknamed "head-on-a-platter". At the height of this fashion, according to one authority, a lady in full dress was obliged to feed herself with a spoon 2 feet long.[1]

[1] Countess of Wilton, *The Art of Needlework*, 1840.

Facsimile page from *A Schole house for the Needle* by Richard Shorleyker, published in 1624, but containing typical Elizabethan motifs. *(From the Victoria & Albert Museum)*

Part of scrolling design
drawn from a late
sixteenth-century coif in
the Victoria and Albert
Museum.
Size reduced by one-third.

Ruffs were first made of fine holland, but the invention of starch made it possible to use much finer qualities of linen, especially lawn and cambric—"such cloth" said Stubbes, referring to cambric, "as the greatest thread shall not be as big as the least hair there is". The manufacture of more and more delicate and transparent fabrics inspired wonder, and often derision. Speaking of lawn, Stowe[1] says "so strange and wonderful was this stuff, that thereupon rose a general scoff or byeword, that shortly they would wear ruffs of a spider's web. . . ." Stubbes, as social commentator and critic, had this to say about the masculine ruff: "They have great and monstrous ruffs made either of cambric, holland, lawn, or some other fine cloth, whereof some be a quarter of a yard deep, some more, and very few less: they stand a full quarter of a yard or more from their necks. . . . Almost none is without them; and everyone, how mean or simple soever they be otherwise, will have of them three or four a-piece for failing; and as though cambrick, holland, lawne, and the finest cloth that can be got anywhere for money, were not good enough, they have them wrought all over with silk work, and peraventure laced with gold and silver and other costly lace . . . and they have now newly found out a more monstrous kind of ruff, of twelve, yea, sixteen lengths a-piece, set three or four times double, and it is of some fitly called 'three steps and a half to the gallows . . .'."[2]

Apart from ruffs, blackwork was highly fashionable on falling-bands, hand-ruffs, handkerchiefs, night-caps and night-shirts. Men's night-caps for sleeping in were plain, but indoors during the day they wore an ornamental cap also called a night-cap, but made of some rich material, such as velvet, with gold and silk embroidery, or of linen, embroidered in a similar fashion, or in blackwork and gold thread. The custom of wearing special night-clothes for sleeping in began in the Tudor period, for until the sixteenth century, men and women slept either naked, or in their daytime shirts and smocks. The Elizabethan nobility favoured embroidered or "wrought night-shirtes" and women also

[1] John Stowe, *Annales of England*, 1580—92, et sequitur.
[2] Philip Stubbes: *Anatomie of Abuses* 1583 (4th ed. 1595).

Late sixteenth-century man's linen night-cap, embroidered in black and white "wrapped" silk in the "flecked" style, with silver-gilt thread, in long-and-short, stem, herringbone and plaited braid stitches, and spangles. The turned-up edge is bordered with silver-gilt lace.

(Courtesy of the Victoria & Albert Museum. Crown copyright)

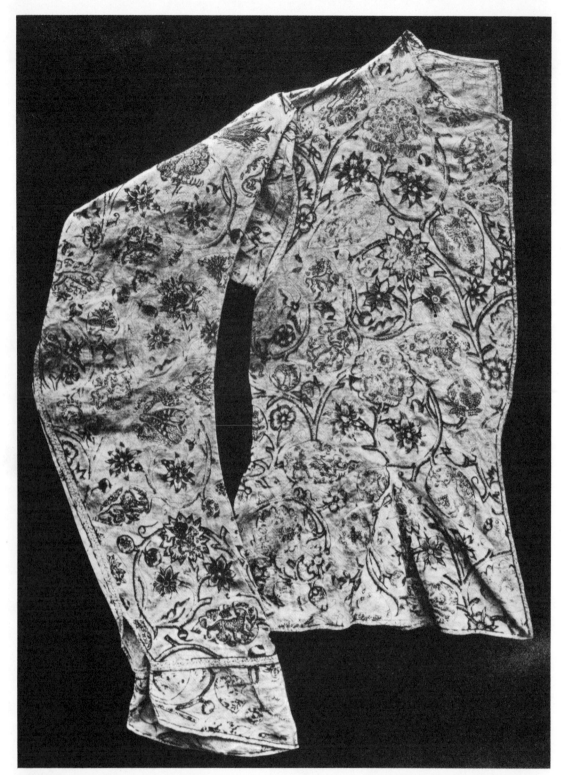

Right front and sleeve of the Falkland Tunic in the Victoria & Albert Museum, given by William IV to the wife of the 10th Viscount Falkland, and said to have belonged to Queen Elizabeth I. Late sixteenth century (*circa* 1586). The left half masked. All seams are embroidered with small diaper patterns.

(*Courtesy of the Victoria & Albert Museum. Crown copyright*)

Some motifs from the Falkland Tunic. Silk embroidery on linen, in stem, back and running stitches and speckling, worked in an all-over pattern of coiling stems bearing outline leaf and flower shapes enclosing many different animals, birds, fishes, etc. fabulous monsters, and little scenes illustrating myths and legends. These copies are true to scale, but the actual embroidery is even finer, in imitation of engraving. Dotted lines show where needle holes have been left after the silk has worn away.

wore in bed, or as négligé, a night-coif, usually in a plain style, and in most cases with a matching frontlet, or "forehead-cloth". This was a triangular piece of material tied round the chin or behind the neck, with the straight edge along the forehead, which on occasion could be smeared with cream to remove wrinkles. Richly embroidered night-coifs were also worn, such as "white cut-work flourished with silver and set with spangells". Day-coifs and forehead-cloths, like men's daytime night-caps, were always embroidered. There is an entry of "Quayffes wroght with black" in an inventory of 1589, in the Essex Record Office.

Early Royal Inventories mention both blackwork *and* Spanish work. In Elizabeth's Great Wardrobe Accounts of 1558–9, there are charges for "overcasting and edging 4 smockes of drawne work with ruffs, wristbands and collars, three of them with blackwork and three of them with red. . . ." (PRO. Nos. 1 & 2). Again, "sixteen yards of Spanish work for ruffs" (Nos. 3 & 4) and "Twelve tooth-cloths with the Spanish stitch, edged with gold and silver bone-lace . . ." (Nos. 5 & 6). Listed among the New Year Gifts elsewhere: "A smock and two pillow-beres of cameryck wrought with blackwork and edged with a broad bone-lace of black silke." "A smock of cameryke wrought with blackwork and edged with bone-lace of gold . . ."; "A smock of cambrik wrought about the collar and sleeves with black silke . . ."; and "From Mistress Twist the Court laundress. Four tooth-cloths of holland, wrought with blackwork and edged with bone-lace of silver and black silk . . .". (Used for rubbing the teeth to clean them, before the advent of the toothbrush. Presumably the working surface was left un-embroidered.)

Women wore either high- or low-necked bodices, and where low, a gathered or embroidered chemise served to cover the bosom, having a standing collar and frill. After 1560, as with the men's style, this began to be superseded by the ruff, and if the chemise was low-necked, the amount of bosom exposed depended on the size and type of ruff worn. Women's ruffs were even vaster and more ornately edged and embroidered than men's. An alternative feminine style to the cartwheel was the fan-shaped ruff, in vogue between 1570 and 1625, mostly worn by unmarried women, in which the ruff rose from the back and sides of a low bodice, spreading out behind the head, and leaving the chest quite uncovered. The partlet, embroidered and jewelled, was still an alternative method of covering up the *décolletage*. It frequently matched the sleeves, in fact matching sets of partlets and detachable sleeves were customary gifts. These detachable sleeves had been a notable feature of Henry VIII's reign, and continued to be very fashionable in Elizabeth's. Sir James Laver comments that their advantage lay not only in adding variety to the costume, but in making it appear that the wearer owned a larger wardrobe than was actually the case. Among Henry VIII's possessions at his death, was an immense number of pairs of sleeves. The "Pelican Portrait" of Queen Elizabeth in the Walker Art Gallery, Liverpool, shows her wearing an open partlet and sleeves in blackwork. Sleeves also often matched the under-skirt or "forepart", an apron-like piece of material inserted into the front opening of the skirt when an undergown was not worn. From 1580, bodices had open fronts filled with a richly decorative stomacher, shaped like an inverted triangle, again often similar to the sleeves. Within its period, Elizabethan dress underwent innumerable modifications of style, impossible to describe within the scope of this book, and recommended as a special study on its own. What concerns us is that blackwork now became an embroidery method for

A forehead cloth, early seventeenth century (Stuart period), worked in long-and-short in the flecked manner with black and white wrapped silk threads. Possibly cut from a larger piece of traced material, as some of the motifs round the edges are incomplete, though more likely the motifs were transferred directly from a page of patterns, those coinciding with the edges of the cloth being unavoidably truncated.

(Courtesy of the Victoria & Albert Museum. Crown copyright)

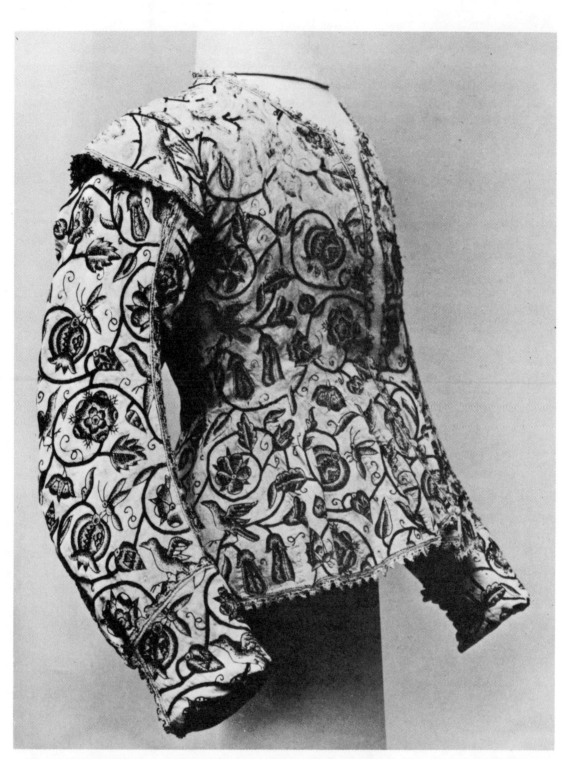

Woman's linen jacket, *circa* 1610–30, from the Isham Collection in the Victoria & Albert Museum, embroidered in the speckling style with stem, braid and back-stitches.

(*Crown copyright*)

outer parts of the dress, as well as for underlinen. It is shown on sleeves, underskirts and stomachers, and when used to decorate them would usually be augmented with jewels, pearls, spangles, and metal threads. A painting of Elizabeth by Gheeraerts, at Hever Castle in Kent, shows the Queen wearing outer sleeves of fine gauze, with inner ones heavily embroidered in blackwork in a meandering floral pattern, interspersed with large jewels.

Domestically, blackwork was a very popular method of decoration for bed-furnishings, coverlets, cushions and curtains, when it was commonly used with gold thread embroidery. The M.S. inventory of the Countess of Shrewsbury at Hardwick mentions: "Three curtins wrought with black silk nedlewerk uppon fine holland cloth". Large-scale items such as bed furnishings which required stiffening and lining were in some instances embroidered and made up in professional workrooms, or by professional embroiderers living as members of the household. These domestic embroideries, and some of the more substantial types of dress embroidery—caps, coifs, jackets, etc., are the first examples of English secular embroidery to survive in any quantity, and can be seen in many museums up and down the country, such as the Falkland Collection in the Victoria and Albert Museum, and the Middleton Collection in Nottingham Castle Museum.

Black and gold repeating pattern *circa* 1600, drawn from a coif in the Victoria and Albert Museum.

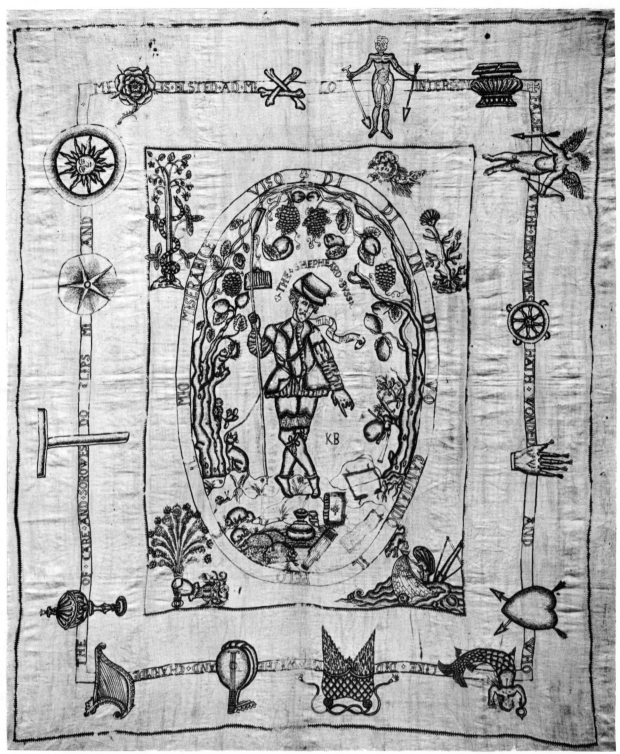

Linen panel, *The Shepheard Buss*, embroidered in Elizabethan blackwork of about 1600. Representing a mourning shepherd surrounded by Latin and Italian mottoes, emblems, and a band of pictographic verse which reads: "False CUPID withe Misfortunes WHEEL hath wonded HAND and HEART who SIREN like did LURE me withe LUTE and charmde HARP the CUP of care and sorowes CROSS do clips mi STAR and SUN mi ROSE is blsted ad mi BONES lo DEATH inters in URN."

(Courtesy of the Victoria & Albert Museum. Crown copyright)

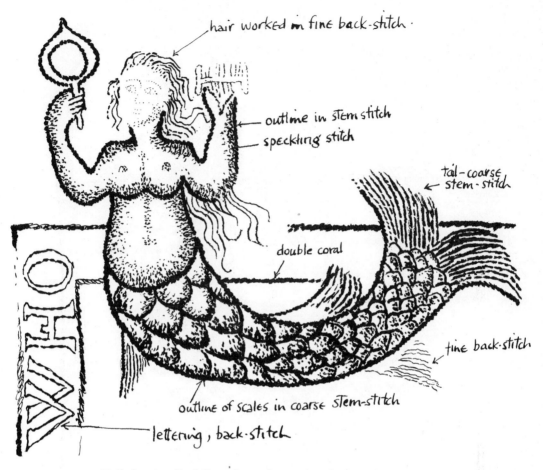

hair worked in fine back-stitch.

outline in stem stitch
speckling stitch

tail-coarse
stem-stitch

double coral

fine back-stitch

outline of scales in coarse stem-stitch

lettering, back-stitch

Full-size detail of Siren figure from *The Shepheard Buss* panel.

Within the method there developed a greater freedom in the use of stitchery, which was worked on the surface of the material, and rarely into the thread, enabling a wider variety of stitches to be employed. Typical stitches used are stem, chain, back-stitch, coral, running, occasionally herringbone and buttonhole, braid stitch for heavy outlines, and plaited braid for metal threads. There is also greater diversity of design matter, which consists sometimes of isolated motifs—fruits, flowers, insects, animals, etc. arranged freely but regularly to make a flat pattern; or, sometimes diverse or repeating motifs as above, within some kind of pattern framework, either geometric, or (very commonly) an arrangement of continuous scrolling stems. Or else the designs are wholly pictorial, taken from book illustrations; although, unlike that of the seventeenth century, sixteenth-century pictorial embroidery, like all Tudor needle-work, always had a practical use and was not produced solely for decoration. Towards the end of this century and at the beginning of the next, designs were being printed directly on to the fabric from engraved plates.

A Jacobean coif, dated sometime in the first half of the seventeenth century, therefore somewhat later than the period with which we are concerned. It is, however, a very good example of a design printed directly on to the linen ground from an engraved plate.
(*Courtesy of the Victoria & Albert Museum. Crown copyright*)

Drawing of part
of a border from a late
sixteenth-century man's night-cap
in the Victoria and Albert Museum.
Fine speckling with stem-stitch outlines on linen.

Four distinct ways of interpreting the designs appear: (1) by diaper fillings with heavy outline, (2) by a "speckling" style, (3) by an engraving style, imitating in thread the actual printed design, (4) by a "flecked" style, produced by working with two threads, a black and a white, twisted together to form a single thread, which imparted a greyish appearance to the work. This method often employed long-and-short stitch. The speckling and flecked styles seem to have been a later development, appearing at the end of the sixteenth and beginning of the seventeenth century.

The scope for employing blackwork as a means of dress decoration increased, as finer and finer qualities of linen became available, and larger and larger quantities went into the construction of ruffs, under-sleeves, and so on, but these materials also made it possible to produce exquisitely fine cutwork and needle-lace, and this became more popular, and indeed, more functional, for ruffs. The main types of linen in use were linen cambric and lawn, widely employed for ruffs, cuffs, collars, kerchiefs, and sometimes smocks. Cobweb-lawn, even finer than these, and linen gauze which was transparent. Also holland in various qualities, principally used for shirts and smocks; lockram, a coarser, loosely woven linen used for shirts, coifs and neckwear by the less wealthy classes, and similarly obtainable in various qualities; and two types of linen used for sheets, a coarse and a fine, called respectively harden and sammeron. For the above information we are indebted to Dr Cunnington. As with the first part of the century, a certain amount was home-produced, but since linen had such an enormous and varied use, a great deal, especially of the finer and more costly varieties, was imported.

The best silk embroidery thread was imported into Europe from the Levant, and from thence to England via the Netherlands. It was sold in skeins of untwisted floss, so many to the pound, and was extremely expensive—in 1511 as much as 2*s.* 6*d.* per ounce, though "black Spanish silk" was somewhat cheaper. Some silk was sold undyed, and home dye-recipes were available for embroideries, though of course they were unable to emulate the brilliant Eastern colours. It may be due to home dyeing, as well as to age, that the black thread of some surviving pieces has faded to a rusty dark-brown. Dye-recipes were very often handed down in the same way as herbal remedies. *The Art of Dying* gives alternative dye recipes for each colour with which it deals. A recipe for black dye is as follows: "Take a quantitie of broken or bruised galles and boyle them in water in a small potte, and when they have a little boyled, take out all the galles, and put into the same potte as much coperas as ye had galles and put therewith a little gumme of Arabye and give it againe another boyling, to let it boyle a little, and with the sayd dye ye shall colour therein your thread, then take it forth, and ye shall see it a faire shining blacke". Another recipe contains more potent ingredients:

> 15 lb of elder bark
> 12 lb of soot (oak shavings or sawdust)
> 10 lb vitriol
> 2 lb wild marjoram
> 6 lb brown-wood
> 1½ lb Calcined Allom and Vitriol mixed
> 4 lb Filings
> as much lye as necessary
> 10 lb Walnut shells

The author feels it incumbent to add "but to either dye a good understanding Artist is necessary".

The gold embroidery thread used with blackwork, known as "silver-gilt", consisted of silver wire coated with a skin of gold, then drawn very fine, and either hammered into strips which were wrapped round silk, or closely spiralled by winding on a special "pirling whele" to make tubular silver-gilt purl. It was also used in its plain wire form as a sewing thread.

Captain Thomas Lee, painted by Marc Gheeraerts the Younger, *circa* 1590. The Captain, described elsewhere as "an Elizabethan thug employed in the Irish Wars"[1] is depicted *en déshabillé*, his open shirt, doublet sleeves and trunk hose all embroidered in blackwork with rose, carnation and honeysuckle motifs.

[1] E. K. Chambers; *Sir Henry Lee*; Oxford, 1936.

ABRIDGED BIBLIOGRAPHY

The Tudor Renaissance, James Lees-Milne. (Batsford, 1951.)

The Tudor Period 1500–1613. (The *Connoisseur*, London, 1956.)

Social England, vol. III, edited by H. D. Traill and J. S. Mann. (Cassell, 1902.)

History of England, vol. I, Froude.

Ciba Review No. 20, vol. 1938–39, A. Wittlin. (Published by Society of Chemical Industries, Basle, Switzerland.)

Naked to Mine Enemies. The Life of Cardinal Wolsey, C. W. Ferguson. (Longmans Green, 1958.)

Costume of the Western World Series—The Tudors to Louis XIII, edited by James Laver. (Harrap & Co., 1952.)

The Art of English Costume, Cunnington. (Collins, 1948, 1949.)

Handbook of English Costume in the Sixteenth Century, C. W. & P. Cunnington. (Faber & Faber, 1954.)

A Dictionary of English Costume, 900–1900, C. W. & P. Cunnington and C. Beard. (A. & C. Black, 1960.)

English Costume, D. Yarwood. (Batsford, 1952.)

Early Pattern-books of Lace, Embroidery and Needlework, E. F. Strange. (London, reprinted by Blades, East & Blades from the Society's *Transactions*, 1904.)

A History of Lace, Mrs Bury Palliser. (Edited 1869. Sampson Low, Son & Marston, London.)

English Domestic Needlework, Hughes. (Lutterworth Press, 1961.)

Catalogue of English Domestic Embroidery, Nevinson. (Victoria & Albert Museum.)

English Art, 1553–1625, E. Mercer. (Clarendon Press, Oxford, 1962.)

Hans Holbein the Younger, Chamberlain. (Geo. Allen & Co., 1913.)

The Paintings of Hans Holbein, Paul Ganz. (Phaidon Press.)

Encyclopedia Britannica.

Chambers's Encyclopedia.

Dictionary of Nat. Biography.

Two

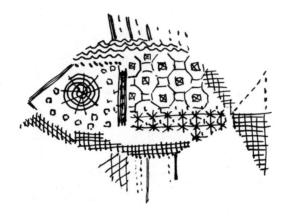

TECHNIQUES TODAY

Transferring the design

AFTER completing the design on paper, it must be transferred to the cloth before embroidery can begin. The method employed will depend on the surface texture of the material, whether rough or smooth. For material with a smooth-textured surface the "prick and pounce" method is most suitable, whereas the tissue paper and tacking method is far more satisfactory for materials with a coarse surface such as some of the heavier linens.

Whichever method is used, begin by ensuring that the outlines of the design are quite clear, and that the material to be used is not wrinkled; iron if necessary. Lay the material on a hard, flat surface such as a board or table.

Prick and pounce method

Equipment required:

    Felt pad (made from a roll of felt and having a flat end).
    Charcoal powder (for light-toned materials).
    French chalk or
    Powdered cuttlefish (for dark-toned materials).
    Weights.
    Pricker or needle.
    Tracing paper or greaseproof paper.
    Fine brush and water colour paint.

1. Trace the outline of the design on to tracing paper.
2. Turn the design on to the *wrong* side, and prick holes round the outlined design. Holes should be small and approximately $\frac{1}{16}$ inch apart.
3. Turn the pricked tracing on to the right side, place it in the correct position on the material, and weight securely.
4. Dip the flat end of the felt pad into the appropriate powder, and work well into the pad on an odd piece of paper. Now rub the pad over the outlines of the design, pressing the pad down firmly and twisting it round in small circular movements. Do not bump the pad up and down as this will result in an indistinct outline.
5. Carefully lift one corner of the design to make sure the design is complete, before removing the tracing.
6. Paint over the powdered outline of the design on the material with a fine paint-brush and watercolour paint and allow to dry thoroughly.

The advantages of this method are that one tracing may be used to repeat the pattern as often as required and the painted outline will remain clear throughout the embroidery.

Charcoal powder and french chalk are available from any chemist.

Paper and tacking method

Equipment required:
    Tissue paper.
    Tacking thread and needle.
1. Trace outline of design on to tissue paper.
2. Using large tacks, secure tissue paper to material at extreme edge.
3. Follow the outline of the design with small running stitches, sewing through paper and material.
4. Remove securing tacks at extreme edge and tear away tissue paper, leaving the design outlined in running stitches.
5. When embroidery is completed take out running stitches.

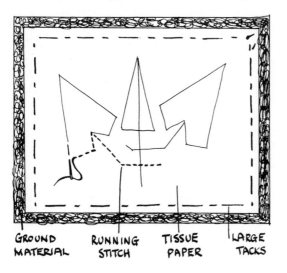

GROUND MATERIAL   RUNNING STITCH   TISSUE PAPER   LARGE TACKS

Tissue paper and tacking method for transferring a design.

Framing

There are so many advantages to be gained from working on a square or slate frame that it is well worth the additional trouble involved; the threads are easier to count when stretched out flat and the work remains cleaner through not being continually crumpled in the hand; when the embroidery is completed it needs little, if any, pressing.

A square frame consists basically of four pieces of wood; two have webbing attached and are called "poles" or "rollers", and two are called "slats" and slot into the poles. Frames can be bought in a variety of sizes, which are measured by the length of the webbing; that is, the width of material that can be mounted. Ideally the frame is balanced between two trestles for working, although some are provided with stands. While embroidering, one hand is kept above the material, and the other below.

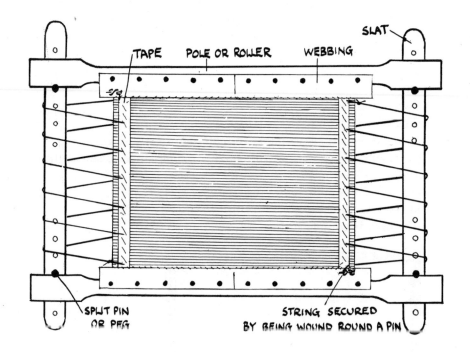

Material mounted in a square or slate frame.

To mount material in a frame

1. Mark the centre of the webbing on both poles permanently, either with a stitch or Indian ink.
2. The material must be exactly on the grain; if necessary pull a thread and cut off any superfluous material.
3. Match the centre of one side of the material to the centre of the webbing on the pole; turn edge of material under about $\frac{1}{4}$ inch and oversew material to webbing with a strong thread, working from the centre to each edge. Repeat on opposite side of material and other pole.
4. Insert the slats in the poles, and stretch lightly.
5. Tack $\frac{1}{2}$ inch tape down the two raw edges of the material, using a diagonal stitch so that it will stretch.

Diagonal tacking stitch for attaching tape when framing.

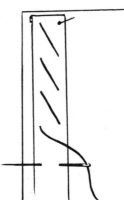

6. Using a coarse needle, thread thin string over the slats and through the centre of the tape at intervals of about $1\frac{1}{4}$ inches, leaving both ends of the string free. When both sides are completed, fasten one end of the string, pull tight to the other end and fasten.
7. Finally, make the material as taut as possible by moving up the pegs, split pins or patent fastening of the slats.

   N.B. If the material is longer than the slats, roll it on to the pole with a layer of tissue paper for protection, unrolling it as required and re-rolling finished work on the opposite pole.

   Circular frames are also available, consisting of two wooden or metal hoops, one fitting inside the other. These are quite suitable for smaller pieces of work, but if moved about on a larger piece of work may mark the material or crush the embroidery. To reduce this tendency to mark, tissue paper may be placed between the hoops and the material, and the inner ring of the frame should be bound with bias binding. The outer ring should have some form of adjustment, usually a screw, which must not be fully tightened until the material is in the frame.

   It is possible to obtain circular frames with a table clamp attachment, so that both hands are free for embroidering as in the slate frame.

Stitches

The basic stitches of blackwork are very simple, but their evenness depends on the ground threads being counted with the utmost accuracy. By counting the threads of the material in varying numbers vertically, horizontally and diagonally, patterns are formed using either back stitch or double running stitch.

It is advisable for the beginner to use back stitch as the pattern may then be built up slowly, bit by bit; but without care this can lead to long stitches on the wrong side which will show through some of the more open even weave materials. If a utilitarian article is being made any long threads will cause the work to be spoilt in laundering.

Back stitch.

Double running stitch, also known as Holbein stitch, is particularly appropriate for border patterns and may even be used for complicated blocks of pattern, but it does require firm concentration and the ability to visualise the completed pattern while working. Double running has the advantage of being neat on the back, obviating the drawbacks of long threads; in the opinion of some workers it can also prove quicker to execute than back stitch.

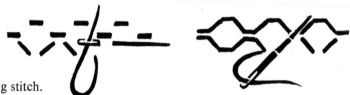

Double running stitch.

Both these stitches have their own advantages and the individual worker will have to experiment with each to find which suits her purpose best. There is no reason why both stitches should not be combined on the same piece of work, double running stitch giving a flowing pattern line and back stitch a more angular effect.

Occasionally included in blackwork fillings is cross stitch, and care must be taken to ensure that the top thread of each cross stitch lies in the same direction.

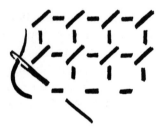

Cross stitch in a blackwork pattern.

Stitches for outlining:

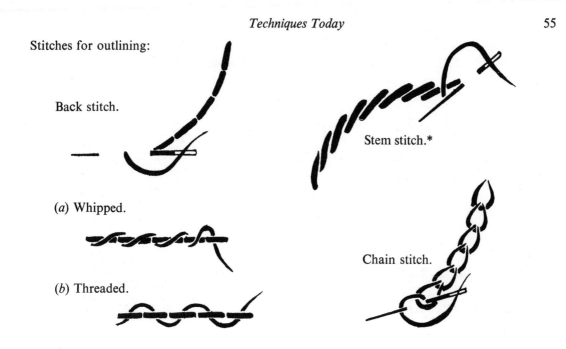

Back stitch.

Stem stitch.*

(*a*) Whipped.

Chain stitch.

(*b*) Threaded.

Many other stitches may be used to outline and connect the filled areas such as back stitch and its variations, chain stitch, stem stitch, coral stitch, pekinese stitch, couching and running stitch.

* Stem stitch should resemble a smooth sleek line when completed; this means bringing the needle up in the hole made by the previous stitch, forming back stitch on the wrong side.

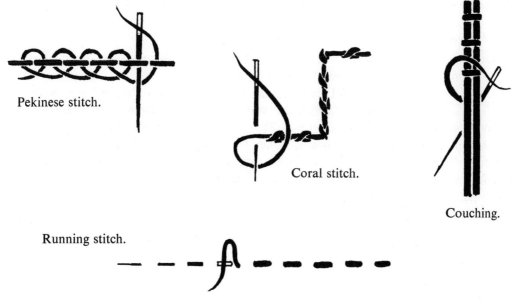

Pekinese stitch.

Coral stitch.

Couching.

Running stitch.

Pattern darning, that is, running stitch over the counted thread to form fillings, may be combined with blackwork fillings to give a more solid effect in places.

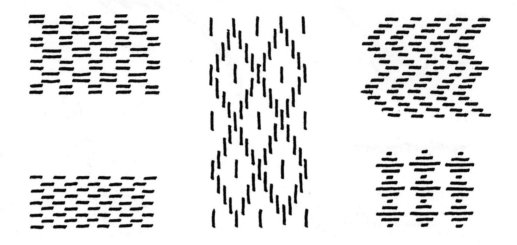

Needles

When working blackwork patterns, it is essential that the needle slides cleanly between the threads of the ground fabric, and therefore the tapestry needle with its blunt point is obviously the best choice. It can be obtained in a range of sizes from the finest, No. 26, to the coarsest, No. 18 (Milwards) and Nos. 26 to 13 (Dryads).

The needle for working any "free" lines will be required to split the threads of the ground, and here the crewel needle is the most suitable; its sizes range from the finest, No. 12, to the largest, No. 1 (Milwards) and Nos. 11 to 1 (Dryads).

Metal threads

Various kinds of metal and imitation metal threads may be combined with blackwork fillings to add richness or to give an effect of liveliness.

Gold, silver, aluminium and Lurex passing threads are all suitable and may be couched in solid areas, or as outlines, or run in and out of the actual fillings to form part of them. The various forms of gold and silver purl, that is, purl purl, check, rough and smooth purl may be cut and sewn on like beads, either following the regularity of the blackwork pattern or "freely". The flat forms of Lurex thread sold on spools for knitting may also be sewn into fillings but should only be used in short lengths, as friction against the eye of the needle tends to make this thread break.

A panel composed of pattern darning and cross stitch, carried out in black, with touches of red and applied gold kid. By EDITH WILLIAMS.

Three

DESIGN

EVERY craft, whether it be fabric printing, pottery or weaving, silversmithing or wood-working, places limitations on the designer by nature of the technical processes which are inherent in that craft. To this embroidery is no exception, and each different method of embroidery imposes varying technical limitations on the designer. Theses on design in general may be read elsewhere, but the aim of this book is to guide the student in one narrow field of embroidery, blackwork.

However, there are certain points which relate to design in general, and which must be given consideration.

Any design applied to an article must form an integral part of that article by being related in size, proportion, colour and fitness, and must not simply form an accessory to it. Therefore the article and its decoration must be considered from the start as one, and not two separate entities. The size, shape and purpose of the article have a very direct bearing on the design that will decorate it and impose limitations on the designer; the technical processes to be used add to these limitations.

Now consider the particular disciplines that blackwork imposes; because it is a method of embroidery worked on the counted thread of a material of very even weave, a certain primness and angularity in the design are inevitable. This is in direct contrast to the modern feeling for "freedom" in working and therefore a compromise has to be reached; as an example, "free" lines worked over the filled areas can make an important contribution to the total design, by linking the patterns together and counteracting their severity; but unless they really do have a meaning within the design, they are best omitted.

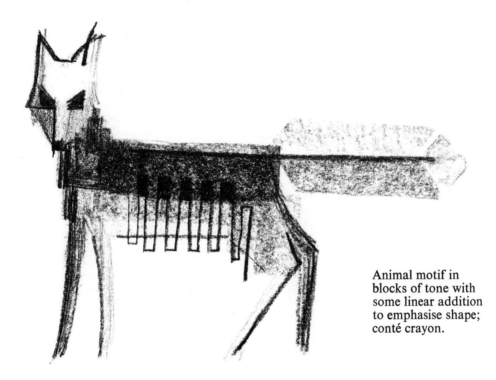

Animal motif in blocks of tone with some linear addition to emphasise shape; conté crayon.

Black and white are absolute opposites, consequently when put beside each other, they produce a dramatic visual contrast. They also create together an effect of severe formality, and it is this formality which is one of the attractions of blackwork.

Between both extremes of black and white lies a progression of greys, resulting from the dilution of one with the other in varying amounts. Blackwork embroidery seeks to exploit, via its particular textile idiom, the same quality of strong contrast linked by intermediate half-tones. It is, in fact, a basic exercise in the use of tone-values, and tonal contrast is its chief ingredient. This can only be achieved by the choice and disposition of the diaper patterns which produce the tones. To define blackwork, therefore, we might describe it as a technique consisting of the juxtaposition of geometric patterns worked into the weave of the material, in order to produce a design composed of areas of dark, medium and light tones.

It is often a problem to decide what subject matter to use for a design, and this is mainly indicated by the purpose of the article to be made, whether purely decorative or utilitarian. No design can be without some foundation in fact, however tenuous, but will be formed by a synthesis of what the designer observes and absorbs; therefore it is necessary for the designer to have a background of reference to act as a stimulant, either in the form of sketchbooks or scrapbooks of cuttings; this is allied to an awareness of the shape of things in everyday life, such as buildings, trees, birds, vehicles, and people.

There is no easy way to create a design, as it can only be formed by an imaginative and experimental approach to the technical requirements of the craft, plus application, concentration and continual practice.

Translating a design from paper to the medium of his craft is the most skilled part of a designer craftsman's work, and needs a sound technical knowledge combined with a willingness to submit to constant self-criticism. The main aim must be to translate the design without losing any spontaneity, and this is particularly difficult in blackwork, which tends towards an extremely "tight" technical method.

Dissected fruit reduced to simple
blocks of tone overlaid with
free lines; conté crayon.

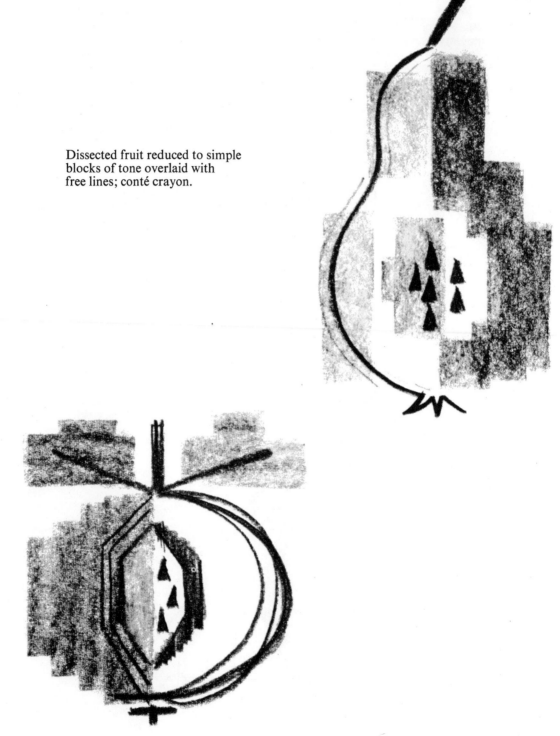

The success of a blackwork design must lie in an emphasis on the importance of areas of tone, and the shapes of these areas in relation to one another. Blackwork designs are essentially composed of areas of flat patterning, and it is the arrangement of these patterns which is really of primary concern. They impart a characteristically formal, flat, static, austere quality to the design. If any misguided designer aims to express movement, naturalism or gay whimsy, this is an even less suitable technique than most, as here the design will be strongly disciplined by the method as in canvas work.

Designs based on thin straggly forms and intricate outlines are unsuited to the method; designs which can be interpreted by means of pattern masses are what is required. The designer is restricted to rather simple shapes, and the skill lies in the subdivision of these shapes into areas of differing proportion and tone.

When designing, it is best to use a medium which suggests tone value. A thick pencil, that is, an architect's pencil with a chisel-pointed, flattened lead, or the side of a piece of conté crayon or pastel chalk on a sheet of rough-grained Whatman paper, will pick up the drawing medium on its surface in varying degrees of intensity. These methods also impart an angularity to the design which can be interpreted more directly into stitchery.

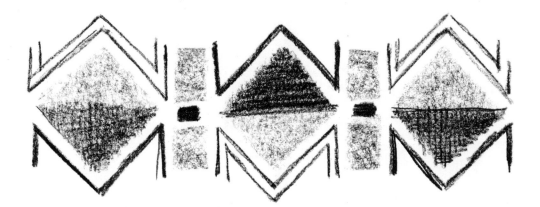

Borders formed of geometric blocks in contrasting tone, with added lines to give a feeling of continuity; conté crayon.

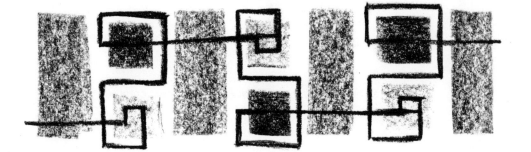

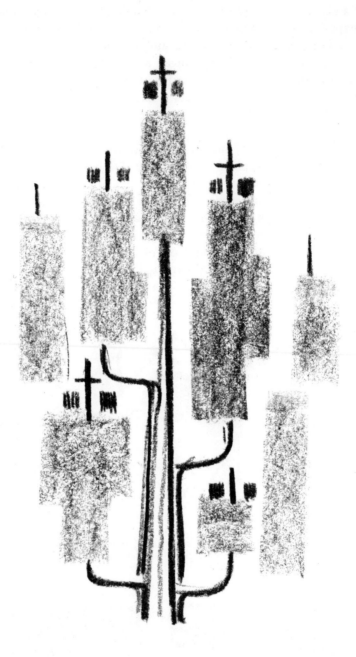

Motifs based on plant, tree and flower forms in conté crayon.

Motif of a bird in conté crayon.

Motif composed of simplified architectural forms in reversed tones of white on black; conté crayon.

Motif of a bird in reverse tones of white on black.

Representation of angel reduced to simple geometric shapes.

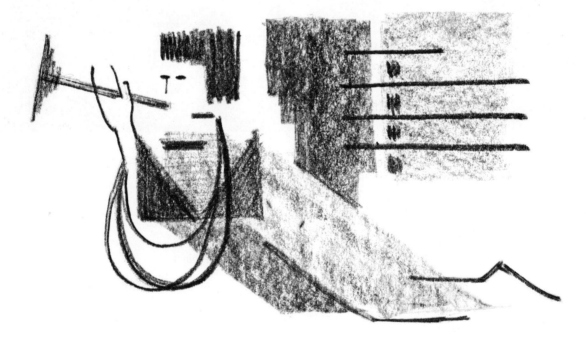

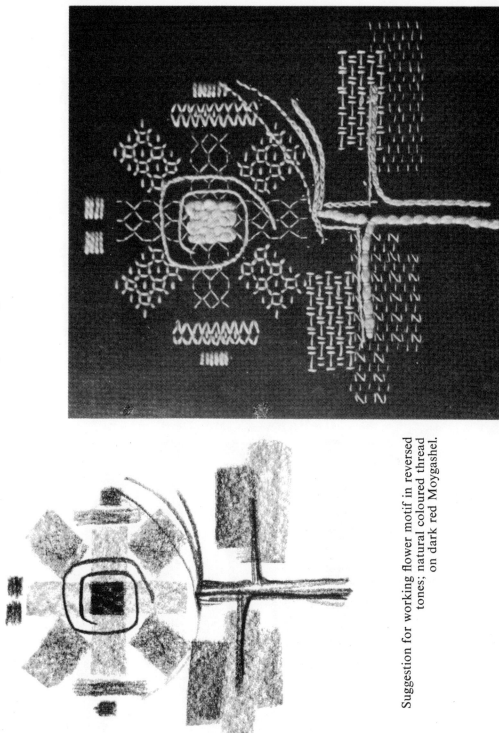

Flower form interpreted in geometric blocks of tone, with added line.

Suggestion for working flower motif in reversed tones; natural coloured thread on dark red Moygashel.

Simple tone relationship as interpreted in cut newspaper.

Simple tone relationship, plus relation of tone to area, as interpreted in cut newspaper.

Another method of design for blackwork is to use a selection of print cuttings from newspapers and magazines, which besides giving a variety of tone values also suggests the pattern of the stitchery. There is the advantage that because newsprint is plentiful and inexpensive, experiments may be made with a variety of shapes without a sense of waste. To produce spontaneous design, cut the shapes directly from the newsprint without any previous drawing; these shapes may then be arranged and rearranged, or discarded, until a satisfactory composition is reached, when the pieces may be stuck to a background.

Free shapes in cut newspaper as an exercise in tone variation, but also composed into an abstract design.

A geometric design consisting only of shapes such as squares, rectangles and diamonds, etc., may have its separate components cut from newsprint and positioned directly on to the ground material. The final arrangement is pinned in position and each shape is outlined with tacking. It may be necessary to count the threads each way of some shapes to ensure accuracy of working. This combines designing and transferring in the minimum number of operations.

Strong tone contrast.

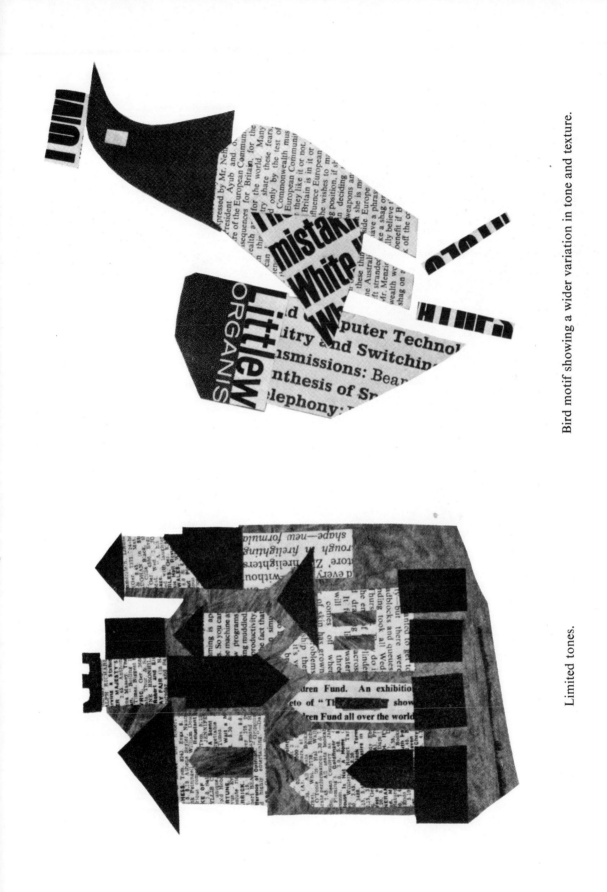

Bird motif showing a wider variation in tone and texture.

Limited tones.

An exercise in designing with cut newspaper—

—and the worked interpretation.
By GLADYS HOPE.

An exercise in designing with cut newspaper—

—and the worked interpretation. By GWEN BLENCOWE.

Colour

It is interesting to try out experiments using coloured patterns instead of the traditional black, but where colours are used, the necessity to exploit the balance of tone values is not altered. The exercise merely becomes more complicated, because now the correct relationship of the colours must be considered as well as that of the tones. These latter are seen at their simplest and most lucid when restricted to black and white, and the addition of colour, unless carefully controlled, will result in destroying the unity and coherence of the design.

With a disciplined choice of colour, however, surprisingly pleasing results may sometimes be achieved; for instance if, on a white ground, two colours related in the colour circle and of the same tone value are chosen, plus a medium and light tone of one of them, thus restricting the total number of colours or tones to four.

A pleasing effect can be produced by contrasting two colours only, the thread being all one colour and the ground another, such as white on turquoise, lemon yellow on dark blue, or dark brown on pale green. An alternative would be to use tones of one colour on another; for example, shades of blue on lime green; maroon shading to pink on grey; mustard shading to olive green on a darkish dull purple. It is necessary that the colour tones are balanced against each other as well as the pattern tones, so that both are integrated happily in the design. Blackwork in colour is robbed of much of its drama and formality; but on the other hand, to break away from the strict traditional line will sometimes result in those pleasant innovations that are the mark of progress.

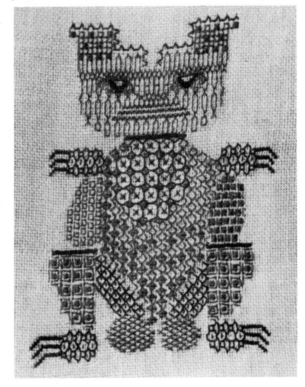

A motif worked
in blue thread.
By ELSIE GUESS.

A fine linen traycloth with blackwork border set within narrow lines of hemstitching. A rust-coloured thread is also used to soften the severity of the black. Designed by E. GEDDES and worked by ANN MCADAM.

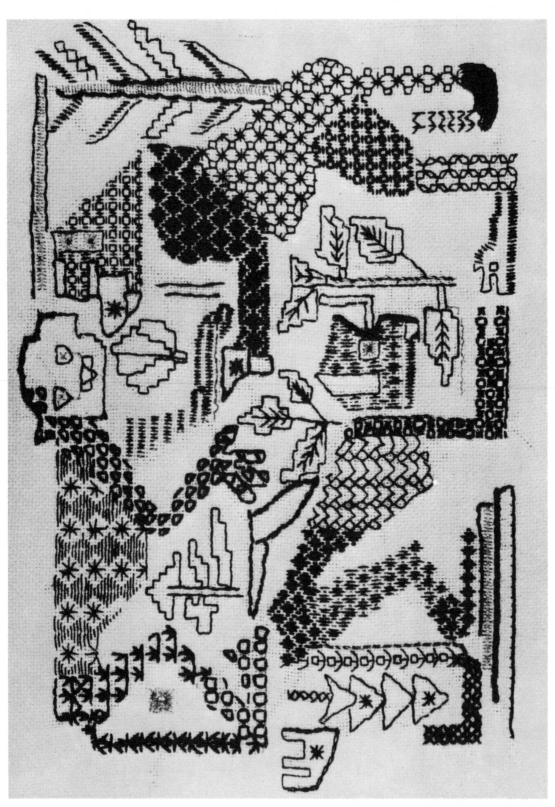

Design of monkey and plant forms.
Worked by KALA DENKAHAR.

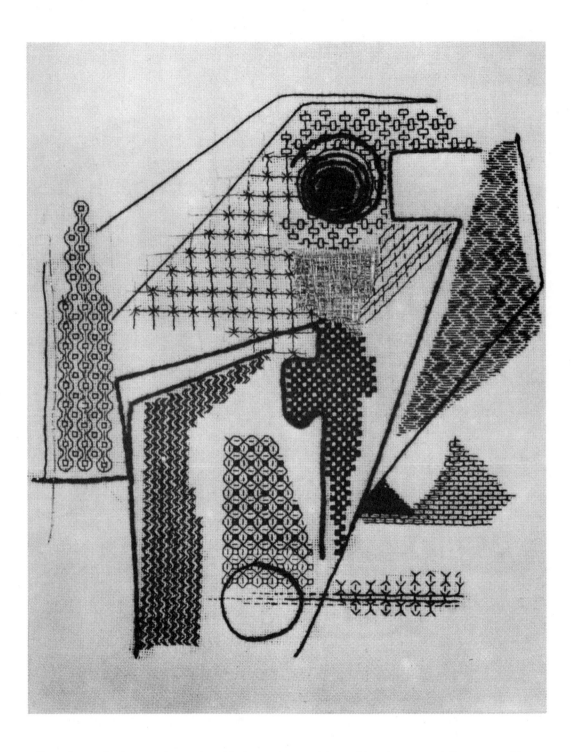

Experiment in free design using black pattern, gold machine Lurex and linear couching.
By PENELOPE HILL.

A cockerel motif, carried out in various thicknesses of thread, including Anchor soft embroidery cotton, coton à broder, and stranded and sewing cottons, with additional patterning in scarlet, and D.M.C. Gold Lurex machine embroidery thread.
Designed and worked by MARGARET DARBY.

Crusader figure designed and worked by NORAH WARD.

A motif which demonstrates stitch direction in blackwork, also the restricted use of outline as a means of emphasising forms, rather than rigidly separating them as shown in the example on page 87—

—and the preliminary sketch using soft pencil to indicate masses of tone. Designed and worked by AUDREY MORRIS.

Four

PATTERNS

GEOMETRIC patterns are the basis of all blackwork, and the selection and arrangement of the patterns needs very careful thought and consideration.

It is not very difficult to invent patterns, basing one's researches on what has gone before. For instance, an existing pattern may be adapted by merely altering its scale, that is, the number of ground threads over which the pattern is worked. Sometimes this changes its appearance completely.

Patterns in the past have been taken from ancient Greek, Roman, and Moorish mosaics and tile designs, and these can still be a fertile source for ideas, also typographic borders, and what are known as "printers' ornaments" or typographical devices.

By doodling on graph paper, many patterns can be built up; a simple exercise is to draw a series of evenly spaced squares, diamonds or triangles on graph paper and then see how they may be linked by horizontal, vertical, and diagonal lines. A wide variety of patterns will result, and by adding further lines, crosses and solid forms, they may be made heavier and more intricate in almost endless permutation.

With the use of different weights of thread a pattern can be enriched or diminished in tone as it is worked. Reducing the thread thickness as the pattern is worked gives it a shaded appearance and helps it to merge gradually into the ground, where this is required by the design. The practice of enclosing every unit of the design, and even each separate area of pattern, within a hard black outline, by now has a very dated appearance, and where such outlines are not absolutely necessary to the design they should be avoided. When such an outline is added, it often helps if the thickness is graduated by varying the working thread. This will prevent it from looking too mechanical, and add liveliness and interest to the work generally.

An interesting blackwork picture of the twenties. The technique has not been allowed to influence the design so that what results is neither true naturalism nor true formalism but a hybrid of both. It contains, however, a great variety of patterns. Worked by DOROTHY HAEGER.

(*From the Permanent Collection of Gray's School of Art, Aberdeen, by courtesy of the Head of School*)

The following pages illustrate a large variety of patterns and some borders; they have purposely not been shown on a graph paper background as the scale of the pattern must always be related both to the design and the size of weave of the ground material. In many patterns the constituent stitches could be worked over 2, 3 or 4 or even 6 threads, and the correct size can only be ascertained by experimenting with a variety of threads on the ground fabric to be used.

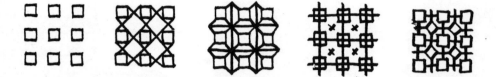

Showing how a simple basis of evenly spaced squares may be built upon to form a variety of patterns. Similarly, any basic geometric shape such as diamonds, triangles or oblongs, can be the starting point for the invention of patterns.

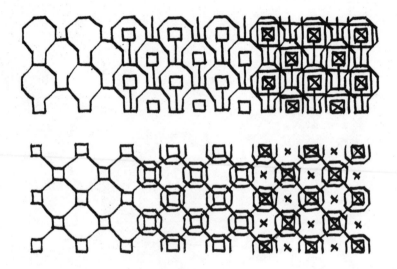

Basically simple patterns can be enriched by the addition of further shapes and lines.

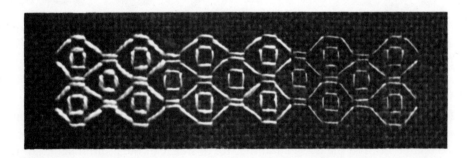

The density of a blackwork pattern may be altered by thickness of thread. Left to right: Sylko Perlé No. 5, coton à broder No. 18, single strand of stranded cotton on coarse Moygashel.

Filling patterns. By removing part of a pattern, e.g. a line, cross or small diamond, the overall effect of the pattern can be completely altered.

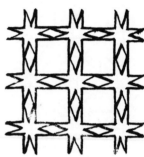

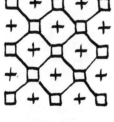

Fillings need not be finished
in meticulous straight lines
but may be tapered off
—see breast of bird motif
opposite.

91

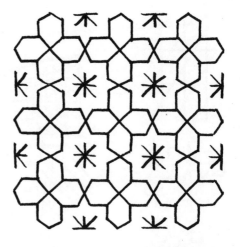

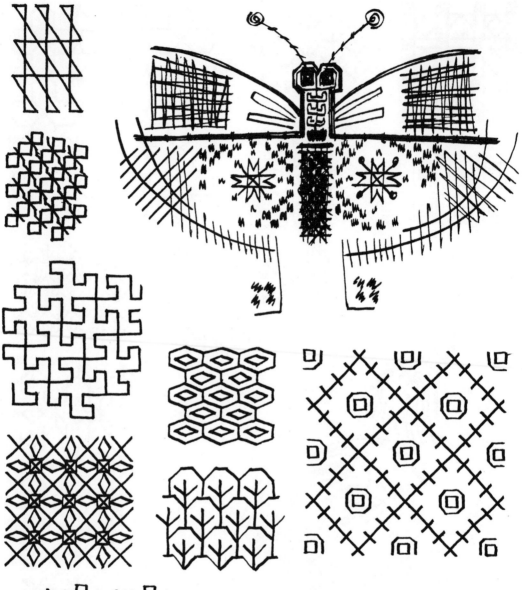

Filling patterns and suggestion for butterfly motif.

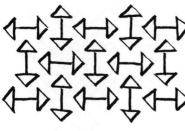

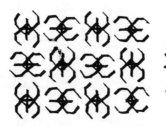

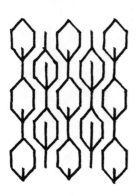

Sections of fillings may
be isolated to form motifs
in their own right.

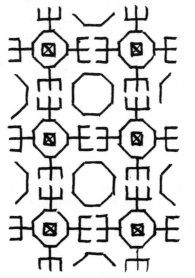

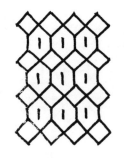

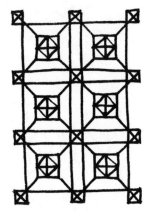

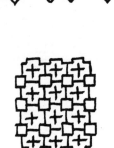

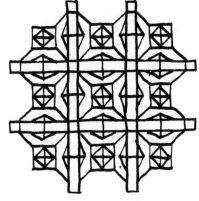

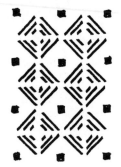

Filling patterns; a strip
of filling pattern can be
detached to form a border.

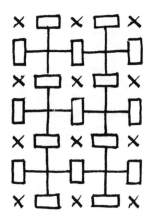

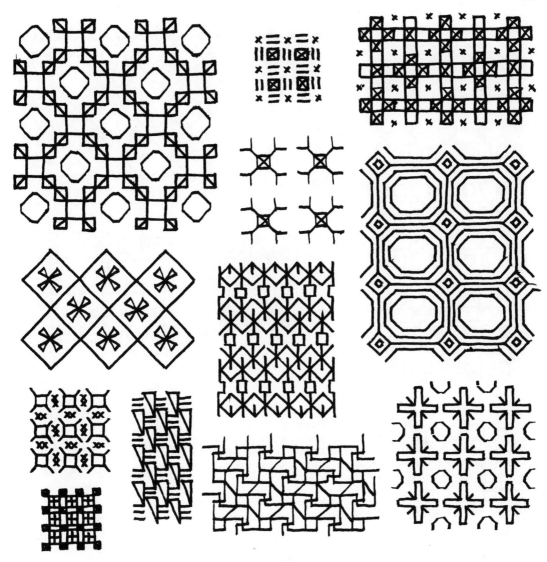

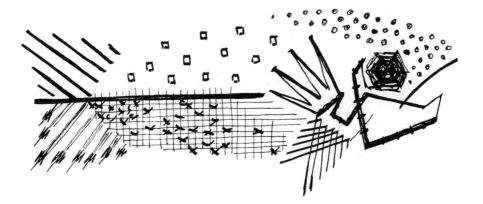

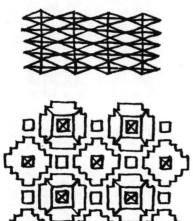

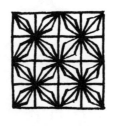

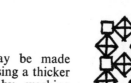

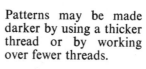

Patterns may be made darker by using a thicker thread or by working over fewer threads.

Sketch motif showing the application of
fillings to a human form.

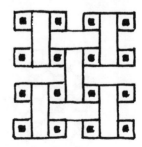

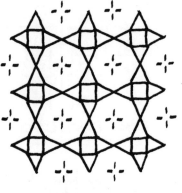

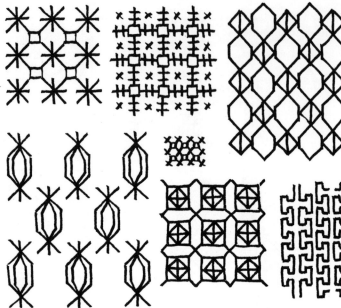

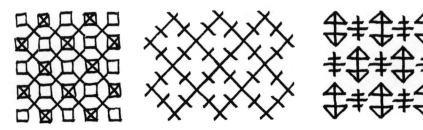

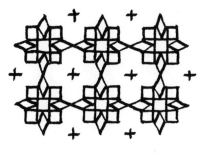

Patterns may be made
lighter in tone by using
a thinner thread or
by working over more
threads.

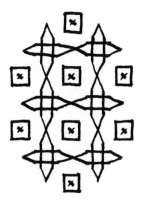

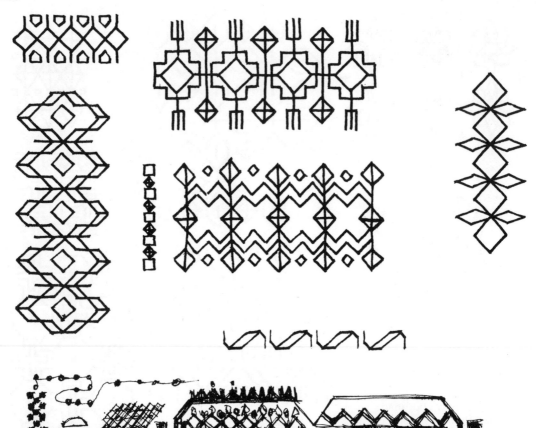

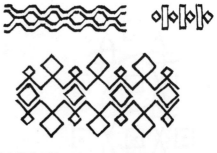

Borders may sometimes be used to advantage in place of filling patterns; the train above shows an idea for their use in this way.

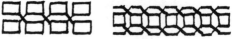

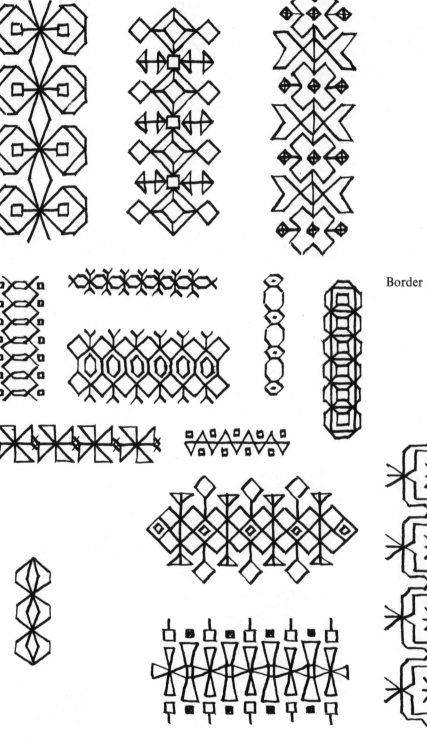

Border patterns.

Borders can be joined together to form filling patterns or split to make small individual motifs.

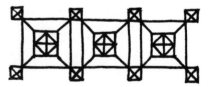

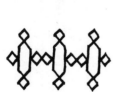

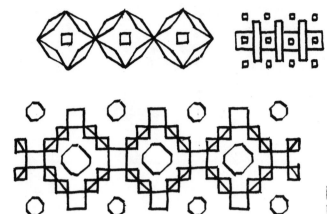

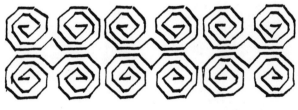

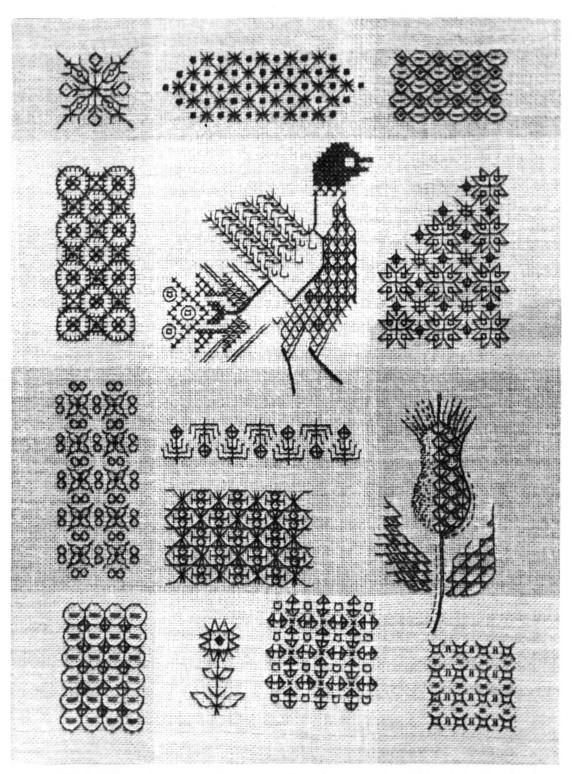

A sampler showing patterns worked on Clunas linen check, and ideas for their application to motifs. Note that blackwork patterns often form sufficient outlines of themselves, as on the thistle and bird. By M. MCNEILL.

More ideas on a sampler of Clunas linen check for patterns and borders, and their employment on motifs. Both samplers were embroidered throughout using only one thickness of thread, coton à broder No. 18. By M. MCNEILL.

Five

MATERIALS AND THREADS

See "Publisher's Note," page 8.

THE geometric patterns which characterise blackwork embroidery require very accurate counting of the warp and weft threads, and therefore it is necessary that the ground fabric should have a precise even weave. Today, not only linens, but cotton and synthetic-fibre materials are available, which are evenly woven. Traditionally, linen is generally recognised as wearing better than modern mercerised cotton or rayon, but where the worker is not averse to departing from rigid tradition, these latter materials offer a wide variety of interesting colours and textures, and save, perhaps, in cases where an exceptionally tough-wearing quality is required, both cotton and rayon are perfectly satisfactory to work on, and usually less expensive than linen.

Blackwork does not necessarily have to be very fine; indeed, striking results can be achieved by working on material with as few as 13–16 threads to the inch. The fineness or otherwise of the material will be governed by the experience and eyesight of the embroiderer, and also the function of the finished work. Fine materials *do* require a greater degree of concentration and patience, as well as very good eyesight. The ultimate end-product is the factor to bear in mind when a ground material is being selected.

There are a wide variety of materials now being manufactured specifically for even-weave embroidery, and the charts beginning on page 108 give details of some of those most suitable for blackwork, arranged in three main groups comprising fine, medium and coarse weaves, governed by the number of threads to the inch.

Less orthodox even-weave materials can sometimes be discovered in the furnishing and dress-fabric departments of big stores. Among these are some of the "Moygashel" fabrics which are manufactured in a wide range of colours and weights. They often have a slub weave, that is, a slight occasional thickness in the yarn, which gives a pleasant texture but makes little difference to the evenness of the worked patterning. On remnant counters, too, it is occasionally possible to find short lengths of material which invite experimental embroidery, and are cheap to buy.

Threads

As blackwork is a monochrome method, it depends for success mainly on the relationship of tone values. The working thread and ground material have each to make their contribution to the quality of the tones produced, and are thus linked together in what might be termed reciprocal partnership. In modern blackwork, the working threads need not be restricted to silk, and any may be used which are found by experiment to work into the material really well and sympathetically.

Generally speaking, the thickness of the working threads should correspond with those of the ground, but one cannot be dogmatic about this, and the worker should use her own discretion, according to the scale and effect required.

It is recommended that a single thread only be used in the needle, in order to keep the stitching precise and even; if a heavier effect is required, it is better to change to a thicker thread, rather than employ several strands of a finer, which may twist and bunch up at the point where they pass through the material.

Suggested threads, from fine to heavy;

Machine Embroidery Cotton, Nos. 50 (very fine) and 30 (less fine).

Perivale Perfection Sewing Silk.

Perivale Imperial Sewing Silk. (This is a fine sewing silk which will split into three strands, which are exceptionally fine, but still strong enough for embroidery.)

Stranded Cotton.

Coton à broder: Clark's D.M.C. and Cartier Bresson in differing weights.

Pearl Cotton, Nos. 5 and 8 (especially for couched outlines).

Anchor Soft (especially for couched outlines).

Ordinary machine sewing cotton can also be used; it has a rounder, harder thread than stranded cotton, and does not readily fluff and thicken through constant passing in and out of the material, which causes gradual blurring and darkening of the pattern. For fine work it will give a very crisp and immaculate effect. The choice of threads is a matter of personal preference and aptitude, but it is advisable when using any soft limp thread, such as stranded cotton, to employ fairly short lengths in the needle. Some materials tend to rub the thread more than others, and this will become evident as the work progresses.

Sewing cottons range in thickness from No. 100, which is fine, through Nos. 60, 40, 36, 24, and 10, a coarse thread. *Metal threads*: see "Techniques Today", page 50.

Blackwork Embroidery

FINE/MEDIUM MATERIALS

Maker	Colour	Name of Material	Approx. No. of threads to one inch	Width in inches
Dryad	Natural, apple green, golden yellow, geranium, scotia grey, coral pink, light delphinium	Willow cross stitch material	30	52
Old Glamis	White	"Lauder" linen gauze	33	50
	Natural	No. 84F brown linen gauze	33	50
	White	No. 842 embroidery linen	27	60
	White	No. 2589 embroidery linen	27	50
Glenshee (Richmond Bros.)	Ivory, cream, natural, buttercup, reseda, wild rose, silver-grey, delphinium	Even-weave linen	29	22, 52
	Natural	Mercerised fabric (quality D)	28	14, 18 22, 39 50
	Geranium, parrot green, azure, golden-brown	Embroidery fabric	27	18, 22 50
Lockhart & Sons	White	634 linen	39	52
	White[1]	6 linen	32	18
	White[1]	596 linen	27	40, 48, 50 60, 62

[1] Lockharts point out that there are colours available in these materials, but they are not necessarily all in stock simultaneously.

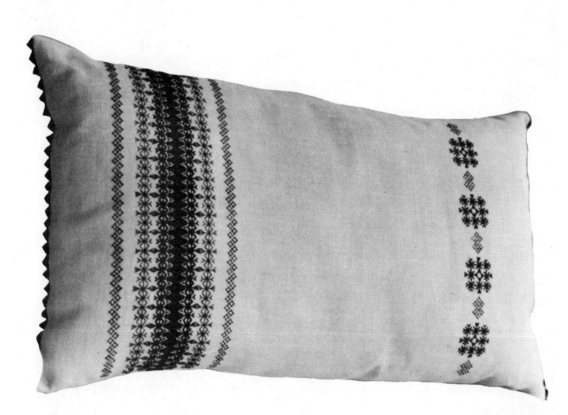

Cushion in grey linen; particularly note the applied black tape sewn down with pale grey thread, which gives added strength to the border. By MRS TAYLOR.

Centre of a tablecloth worked on Old Glamis 274 linen in varying thicknesses of coton à broder, white on turquoise; The embroidery is worked in double running stitch throughout. This is the kind of design that may be counted directly on to the material from only a basic sketch idea. By M. MCNEILL.

MEDIUM/COARSE MATERIALS

MAKER	COLOUR	NAME OF MATERIAL	APPROX. NO. OF THREADS TO ONE INCH	WIDTH IN INCHES
Old Glamis	Ivory, natural	No. 274 embroidery linen	22	22, 50
	Pale green, pale and royal blue, pink, jade, yellow, dark brown, grey, vermilion, turquoise	No. 274 embroidery linen	22	50
	4 inch check: Natural/white, green/white, yellow/white, blue/white, rose/white	"Clunas" linen check	25	52
Glenshee (Richmond Bros.)	Ivory, yellow, jade, red, grey, royal blue	Even-weave linen S.P. quality	25	22 ivory only. 50 all shades
Lockhart & Sons	White[1]	595 linen	21	28, 40, 48, 56, 59½, 67

[1] Lockharts point out that there are colours available in these materials, but they are not necessarily all in stock simultaneously.

COARSE MATERIALS

MAKER	COLOUR	NAME OF MATERIAL	APPROX. NO. OF THREADS TO ONE INCH	WIDTH IN INCHES
Dryad	Natural	Coarse willow cross stitch material	18	50
Old Glamis	Ivory	"Peebles" cloth	17	14, 18, 22
	White	841 embroidery linen	19	55
	Natural/white mixture	No. 261 linen 05160	15	50
	Pale brown/white mixture	Raeburn crash	16	22, 34, 50
	Pale brown/white mixture	"Titian" cloth	13	20, 50
	Mixtures: blues, browns, oranges, jade, yellow, green, pink, black	"Titian" cloth	13	50
	Oatmeal/white mixture	"Rosemount" crash	13	48
Glenshee (Richmond Bros.)	Natural	Embroidery fabric (quality 99)	17	14, 22
	Natural/white	Embroidery fabric (quality 20X)	19	14, 18, 22, 50
	Natural	Embroidery fabric (quality 22X)	18	14, 18, 22, 50
	Natural	Mercerised fabric (quality A)	17	14, 18, 22, 50
	Natural	Mercerised fabric (quality C)	18	14, 18, 22, 50

COARSE MATERIALS (*contd.*)

MAKER	COLOUR	NAME OF MATERIALS	APPROX. NO. OF THREADS TO ONE INCH	WIDTH IN INCHES
Glenshee (Richmond Bros.)	Natural	Linen	18	14, 18, 22, 50
	Oatmeal	Linen	18	14, 18, 22, 50
Lockhart & Sons	White	217 linen	19	28, 36, 40, 43¼, 48, 51, 55, 56, 60, 63, 72, 73
	White	737 linen	17	56, 60, 63

As it is sometimes difficult to obtain a particular material in local shops, the following are suppliers specialising in orders of embroidery materials by post, and can be strongly recommended; a catalogue or samples will be sent on receipt of a stamped addressed envelope.

Mace & Nairn, 89 Crane Street, Salisbury, Wiltshire (stockists of a very wide range of even-weave materials and metal threads).

Mrs Mary Allen, Turnditch, Derbyshire (even-weave materials and a wide variety of threads).

The Rambler Studio, Holford, Somerset (even-weave materials).

Dryad Handicrafts have premises at: Northgates, Leicester, and will supply orders by post.

The following manufacturers will supply information concerning their stockists, should difficulty be found in obtaining their fabrics:

L. Lockhart & Sons, Ltd, Linktown Works, Kirkaldy, Fife, Scotland.

Donald Bros., Old Glamis Factory, Dundee, Scotland.

Richmond Bros., Balfield Road Works, Dundee, Scotland.

The above addresses are listed as being convenient for ordering by post for those living out of town, and it is assumed that the reader will be familiar with London stockists of embroidery materials such as Harrods, the Needlewoman Shop, the Royal School of Needlework and shops and suppliers in other cities in Britain.

Embroidered on a white Glenshee linen in a wide variety of black threads, with small amounts of Lurex and metal threads original size 30 by 15 inches. by M. MCNEILL.

By kind permission of the Principal, King Alfred's College, Winchester, and Miss Elaine Price.

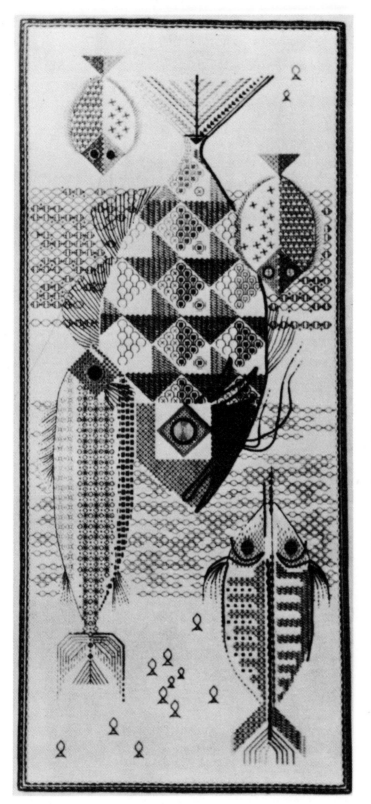

Two interpretations of the same design. After the first panel had been worked the designer felt it was too "tight" in appearance, and therefore worked the second panel using the same basic design, blackwork patterns and threads, but breaking the outlines and patterns to give a more fluid effect in keeping with the marine subject matter.

A CATALOGUE OF SELECTED DOVER BOOKS
IN ALL FIELDS OF INTEREST

AMERICA'S OLD MASTERS, James T. Flexner. Four men emerged unexpectedly from provincial 18th century America to leadership in European art: Benjamin West, J. S. Copley, C. R. Peale, Gilbert Stuart. Brilliant coverage of lives and contributions. Revised, 1967 edition. 69 plates. 365pp. of text.

21806-6 Paperbound $3.00

FIRST FLOWERS OF OUR WILDERNESS: AMERICAN PAINTING, THE COLONIAL PERIOD, James T. Flexner. Painters, and regional painting traditions from earliest Colonial times up to the emergence of Copley, West and Peale Sr., Foster, Gustavus Hesselius, Feke, John Smibert and many anonymous painters in the primitive manner. Engaging presentation, with 162 illustrations. xxii + 368pp.

22180-6 Paperbound $3.50

THE LIGHT OF DISTANT SKIES: AMERICAN PAINTING, 1760-1835, James T. Flexner. The great generation of early American painters goes to Europe to learn and to teach: West, Copley, Gilbert Stuart and others. Allston, Trumbull, Morse; also contemporary American painters—primitives, derivatives, academics—who remained in America. 102 illustrations. xiii + 306pp.   22179-2 Paperbound $3.50

A HISTORY OF THE RISE AND PROGRESS OF THE ARTS OF DESIGN IN THE UNITED STATES, William Dunlap. Much the richest mine of information on early American painters, sculptors, architects, engravers, miniaturists, etc. The only source of information for scores of artists, the major primary source for many others. Unabridged reprint of rare original 1834 edition, with new introduction by James T. Flexner, and 394 new illustrations. Edited by Rita Weiss. 6⅝ x 9⅝.

21695-0, 21696-9, 21697-7 Three volumes, Paperbound $15.00

EPOCHS OF CHINESE AND JAPANESE ART, Ernest F. Fenollosa. From primitive Chinese art to the 20th century, thorough history, explanation of every important art period and form, including Japanese woodcuts; main stress on China and Japan, but Tibet, Korea also included. Still unexcelled for its detailed, rich coverage of cultural background, aesthetic elements, diffusion studies, particularly of the historical period. 2nd, 1913 edition. 242 illustrations. lii + 439pp. of text.

20364-6, 20365-4 Two volumes, Paperbound $6.00

THE GENTLE ART OF MAKING ENEMIES, James A. M. Whistler. Greatest wit of his day deflates Oscar Wilde, Ruskin, Swinburne; strikes back at inane critics, exhibitions, art journalism; aesthetics of impressionist.revolution in most striking form. Highly readable classic by great painter. Reproduction of edition designed by Whistler. Introduction by Alfred Werner. xxxvi + 334pp.

21875-9 Paperbound $3.00

DESIGN BY ACCIDENT; A BOOK OF "ACCIDENTAL EFFECTS" FOR ARTISTS AND DESIGNERS, James F. O'Brien. Create your own unique, striking, imaginative effects by "controlled accident" interaction of materials: paints and lacquers, oil and water based paints, splatter, crackling materials, shatter, similar items. Everything you do will be different; first book on this limitless art, so useful to both fine artist and commercial artist. Full instructions. 192 plates showing "accidents," 8 in color. viii + 215pp. 8⅜ x 11¼.   21942-9 Paperbound $3.75

THE BOOK OF SIGNS, Rudolf Koch. Famed German type designer draws 493 beautiful symbols: religious, mystical, alchemical, imperial, property marks, runes, etc. Remarkable fusion of traditional and modern. Good for suggestions of timelessness, smartness, modernity. Text. vi + 104pp. 6⅛ x 9¼.
                                        20162-7 Paperbound $1.50

HISTORY OF INDIAN AND INDONESIAN ART, Ananda K. Coomaraswamy. An unabridged republication of one of the finest books by a great scholar in Eastern art. Rich in descriptive material, history, social backgrounds; Sunga reliefs, Rajput paintings, Gupta temples, Burmese frescoes, textiles, jewelry, sculpture, etc. 400 photos. viii + 423pp. 6⅜ x 9¾.   21436-2 Paperbound $5.00

PRIMITIVE ART, Franz Boas. America's foremost anthropologist surveys textiles, ceramics, woodcarving, basketry, metalwork, etc.; patterns, technology, creation of symbols, style origins. All areas of world, but very full on Northwest Coast Indians. More than 350 illustrations of baskets, boxes, totem poles, weapons, etc. 378 pp.
                                        20025-6 Paperbound $3.00

THE GENTLEMAN AND CABINET MAKER'S DIRECTOR, Thomas Chippendale. Full reprint (third edition, 1762) of most influential furniture book of all time, by master cabinetmaker. 200 plates, illustrating chairs, sofas, mirrors, tables, cabinets, plus 24 photographs of surviving pieces. Biographical introduction by N. Bienenstock. vi + 249pp. 9⅞ x 12¾.   21601-2 Paperbound $5.00

AMERICAN ANTIQUE FURNITURE, Edgar G. Miller, Jr. The basic coverage of all American furniture before 1840. Individual chapters cover type of furniture—clocks, tables, sideboards, etc.—chronologically, with inexhaustible wealth of data. More than 2100 photographs, all identified, commented on. Essential to all early American collectors. Introduction by H. E. Keyes. vi + 1106pp. 7⅞ x 10¾.
                    21599-7, 21600-4 Two volumes, Paperbound $11.00

PENNSYLVANIA DUTCH AMERICAN FOLK ART, Henry J. Kauffman. 279 photos, 28 drawings of tulipware, Fraktur script, painted tinware, toys, flowered furniture, quilts, samplers, hex signs, house interiors, etc. Full descriptive text. Excellent for tourist, rewarding for designer, collector. Map. 146pp. 7⅞ x 10¾.
                                        21205-X Paperbound $3.00

EARLY NEW ENGLAND GRAVESTONE RUBBINGS, Edmund V. Gillon, Jr. 43 photographs, 226 carefully reproduced rubbings show heavily symbolic, sometimes macabre early gravestones, up to early 19th century. Remarkable early American primitive art, occasionally strikingly beautiful; always powerful. Text. xxvi + 207pp. 8⅜ x 11¼.   21380-3 Paperbound $4.00

A History of Costume, Carl Köhler. Definitive history, based on surviving pieces of clothing primarily, and paintings, statues, etc. secondarily. Highly readable text, supplemented by 594 illustrations of costumes of the ancient Mediterranean peoples, Greece and Rome, the Teutonic prehistoric period; costumes of the Middle Ages, Renaissance, Baroque, 18th and 19th centuries. Clear, measured patterns are provided for many clothing articles. Approach is practical throughout. Enlarged by Emma von Sichart. 464pp. 21030-8 Paperbound $3.50

Oriental Rugs, Antique and Modern, Walter A. Hawley. A complete and authoritative treatise on the Oriental rug—where they are made, by whom and how, designs and symbols, characteristics in detail of the six major groups, how to distinguish them and how to buy them. Detailed technical data is provided on periods, weaves, warps, wefts, textures, sides, ends and knots, although no technical background is required for an understanding. 11 color plates, 80 halftones, 4 maps. vi + 320pp. 6⅛ x 9⅛. 22366-3 Paperbound $5.00

Ten Books on Architecture, Vitruvius. By any standards the most important book on architecture ever written. Early Roman discussion of aesthetics of building, construction methods, orders, sites, and every other aspect of architecture has inspired, instructed architecture for about 2,000 years. Stands behind Palladio, Michelangelo, Bramante, Wren, countless others. Definitive Morris H. Morgan translation. 68 illustrations. xii + 331pp. 20645-9 Paperbound .$3.00

The Four Books of Architecture, Andrea Palladio. Translated into every major Western European language in the two centuries following its publication in 1570, this has been one of the most influential books in the history of architecture. Complete reprint of the 1738 Isaac Ware edition. New introduction by Adolf Placzek, Columbia Univ. 216 plates. xxii + 110pp. of text. 9½ x 12¾. 21308-0 Clothbound $12.50

Sticks and Stones: A Study of American Architecture and Civilization, Lewis Mumford.One of the great classics of American cultural history. American architecture from the medieval-inspired earliest forms to the early 20th century; evolution of structure and style, and reciprocal influences on environment. 21 photographic illustrations. 238pp. 20202-X Paperbound $2.00

The American Builder's Companion, Asher Benjamin. The most widely used early 19th century architectural style and source book, for colonial up into Greek Revival periods. Extensive development of geometry of carpentering, construction of sashes, frames, doors, stairs; plans and elevations of domestic and other buildings. Hundreds of thousands of houses were built according to this book, now invaluable to historians, architects, restorers, etc. 1827 edition. 59 plates. 114pp. 7⅞ x 10¾. 22236-5 Paperbound $4.00

Dutch Houses in the Hudson Valley Before 1776, Helen Wilkinson Reynolds. The standard survey of the Dutch colonial house and outbuildings, with constructional features, decoration, and local history associated with individual homesteads. Introduction by Franklin D. Roosevelt. Map. 150 illustrations. 469pp. 6⅝ x 9¼. 21469-9 Paperbound $5.00

POEMS OF ANNE BRADSTREET, edited with an introduction by Robert Hutchinson. A new selection of poems by America's first poet and perhaps the first significant woman poet in the English language. 48 poems display her development in works of considerable variety—love poems, domestic poems, religious meditations, formal elegies, "quaternions," etc. Notes, bibliography. viii + 222pp.

22160-1 Paperbound $2.50

THREE GOTHIC NOVELS: THE CASTLE OF OTRANTO BY HORACE WALPOLE; VATHEK BY WILLIAM BECKFORD; THE VAMPYRE BY JOHN POLIDORI, WITH FRAGMENT OF A NOVEL BY LORD BYRON, edited by E. F. Bleiler. The first Gothic novel, by Walpole; the finest Oriental tale in English, by Beckford; powerful Romantic supernatural story in versions by Polidori and Byron. All extremely important in history of literature; all still exciting, packed with supernatural thrills, ghosts, haunted castles, magic, etc. xl + 291pp.

21232-7 Paperbound $3.00

THE BEST TALES OF HOFFMANN, E. T. A: Hoffmann. 10 of Hoffmann's most important stories, in modern re-editings of standard translations: Nutcracker and the King of Mice, Signor Formica, Automata, The Sandman, Rath Krespel, The Golden Flowerpot, Master Martin the Cooper, The Mines of Falun, The King's Betrothed, A New Year's Eve Adventure. 7 illustrations by Hoffmann. Edited by E. F. Bleiler. xxxix + 419pp. 21793-0 Paperbound $3.00

GHOST AND HORROR STORIES OF AMBROSE BIERCE, Ambrose Bierce. 23 strikingly modern stories of the horrors latent in the human mind: The Eyes of the Panther, The Damned Thing, An Occurrence at Owl Creek Bridge, An Inhabitant of Carcosa, etc., plus the dream-essay, Visions of the Night. Edited by E. F. Bleiler. xxii + 199pp. 20767-6 Paperbound $2.00

BEST GHOST STORIES OF J. S. LEFANU, J. Sheridan LeFanu. Finest stories by Victorian master often considered greatest supernatural writer of all. Carmilla, Green Tea, The Haunted Baronet, The Familiar, and 12 others. Most never before available in the U. S. A. Edited by E. F. Bleiler. 8 illustrations from Victorian publications. xvii + 467pp. 20415-4 Paperbound $3.00

MATHEMATICAL FOUNDATIONS OF INFORMATION THEORY, A. I. Khinchin. Comprehensive introduction to work of Shannon, McMillan, Feinstein and Khinchin, placing these investigations on a rigorous mathematical basis. Covers entropy concept in probability theory, uniqueness theorem, Shannon's inequality, ergodic sources, the E property, martingale concept, noise, Feinstein's fundamental lemma, Shanon's first and second theorems. Translated by R. A. Silverman and M. D. Friedman. iii + 120pp. 60434-9 Paperbound $2.00

SEVEN SCIENCE FICTION NOVELS, H. G. Wells. The standard collection of the great novels. Complete, unabridged. *First Men in the Moon, Island of Dr. Moreau, War of the Worlds, Food of the Gods, Invisible Man, Time Machine, In the Days of the Comet.* Not only science fiction fans, but every educated person owes it to himself to read these novels. 1015pp. (USO) 20264-X Clothbound $6.00

AMERICAN FOOD AND GAME FISHES, David S. Jordan and Barton W. Evermann. Definitive source of information, detailed and accurate enough to enable the sportsman and nature lover to identify conclusively some 1,000 species and sub-species of North American fish, sought for food or sport. Coverage of range, physiology, habits, life history, food value. Best methods of capture, interest to the angler, advice on bait, fly-fishing, etc. 338 drawings and photographs. l + 574pp. 6⅝ x 9⅜.
22196-2 Paperbound $5.00

THE FROG BOOK, Mary C. Dickerson. Complete with extensive finding keys, over 300 photographs, and an introduction to the general biology of frogs and toads, this is the classic non-technical study of Northeastern and Central species. 58 species; 290 photographs and 16 color plates. xvii + 253pp.
21973-9 Paperbound $4.00

THE MOTH BOOK: A GUIDE TO THE MOTHS OF NORTH AMERICA, William J. Holland. Classical study, eagerly sought after and used for the past 60 years. Clear identification manual to more than 2,000 different moths, largest manual in existence. General information about moths, capturing, mounting, classifying, etc., followed by species by species descriptions. 263 illustrations plus 48 color plates show almost every species, full size. 1968 edition, preface, nomenclature changes by A. E. Brower. xxiv + 479pp. of text. 6½ x 9¼.
21948-8 Paperbound $6.00

THE SEA-BEACH AT EBB-TIDE, Augusta Foote Arnold. Interested amateur can identify hundreds of marine plants and animals on coasts of North America; marine algae; seaweeds; squids; hermit crabs; horse shoe crabs; shrimps; corals; sea anemones; etc. Species descriptions cover: structure; food; reproductive cycle; size; shape; color; habitat; etc. Over 600 drawings. 85 plates. xii + 490pp.
21949-6 Paperbound $4.00

COMMON BIRD SONGS, Donald J. Borror. 33⅓ 12-inch record presents songs of 60 important birds of the eastern United States. A thorough, serious record which provides several examples for each bird, showing different types of song, individual variations, etc. Inestimable identification aid for birdwatcher. 32-page booklet gives text about birds and songs, with illustration for each bird.
21829-5 Record, book, album. Monaural. $3.50

FADS AND FALLACIES IN THE NAME OF SCIENCE, Martin Gardner. Fair, witty appraisal of cranks and quacks of science: Atlantis, Lemuria, hollow earth, flat earth, Velikovsky, orgone energy, Dianetics, flying saucers, Bridey Murphy, food fads, medical fads, perpetual motion, etc. Formerly "In the Name of Science." x + 363pp.
20394-8 Paperbound $3.00

HOAXES, Curtis D. MacDougall. Exhaustive, unbelievably rich account of great hoaxes: Locke's moon hoax, Shakespearean forgeries, sea serpents, Loch Ness monster, Cardiff giant, John Wilkes Booth's mummy, Disumbrationist school of art, dozens more; also journalism, psychology of hoaxing. 54 illustrations. xi + 338pp.
20465-0 Paperbound $3.50

ALPHABETS AND ORNAMENTS, Ernst Lehner. Well-known pictorial source for decorative alphabets, script examples, cartouches, frames, decorative title pages, calligraphic initials, borders, similar material. 14th to 19th century, mostly European. Useful in almost any graphic arts designing, varied styles. 750 illustrations. 256pp. 7 x 10.   21905-4 Paperbound $4.00

PAINTING: A CREATIVE APPROACH, Norman Colquhoun. For the beginner simple guide provides an instructive approach to painting: major stumbling blocks for beginner; overcoming them, technical points; paints and pigments; oil painting; watercolor and other media and color. New section on "plastic" paints. Glossary. Formerly *Paint Your Own Pictures.* 221pp.   22000-1 Paperbound $1.75

THE ENJOYMENT AND USE OF COLOR, Walter Sargent. Explanation of the relations between colors themselves and between colors in nature and art, including hundreds of little-known facts about color values, intensities, effects of high and low illumination, complementary colors. Many practical hints for painters, references to great masters. 7 color plates, 29 illustrations. x + 274pp.
                                                                          20944-X Paperbound $3.00

THE NOTEBOOKS OF LEONARDO DA VINCI, compiled and edited by Jean Paul Richter. 1566 extracts from original manuscripts reveal the full range of Leonardo's versatile genius: all his writings on painting, sculpture, architecture, anatomy, astronomy, geography, topography, physiology, mining, music, etc., in both Italian and English, with 186 plates of manuscript pages and more than 500 additional drawings. Includes studies for the Last Supper, the lost Sforza monument, and other works. Total of xlvii + 866pp. 7⅞ x 10¾.
                                    22572-0, 22573-9 Two volumes, Paperbound $12.00

MONTGOMERY WARD CATALOGUE OF 1895. Tea gowns, yards of flannel and pillow-case lace, stereoscopes, books of gospel hymns, the New Improved Singer Sewing Machine, side saddles, milk skimmers, straight-edged razors, high-button shoes, spittoons, and on and on . . . listing some 25,000 items, practically all illustrated. Essential to the shoppers of the 1890's, it is our truest record of the spirit of the period. Unaltered reprint of Issue No. 57, Spring and Summer 1895. Introduction by Boris Emmet. Innumerable illustrations. xiii + 624pp. 8½ x 11⅝.
                                                                          22377-9 Paperbound $8.50

THE CRYSTAL PALACE EXHIBITION ILLUSTRATED CATALOGUE (LONDON, 1851). One of the wonders of the modern world—the Crystal Palace Exhibition in which all the nations of the civilized world exhibited their achievements in the arts and sciences—presented in an equally important illustrated catalogue. More than 1700 items pictured with accompanying text—ceramics, textiles, cast-iron work, carpets, pianos, sleds, razors, wall-papers, billiard tables, beehives, silverware and hundreds of other artifacts—represent the focal point of Victorian culture in the Western World. Probably the largest collection of Victorian decorative art ever assembled— indispensable for antiquarians and designers. Unabridged republication of the Art-Journal Catalogue of the Great Exhibition of 1851, with all terminal essays. New introduction by John Gloag, F.S.A. xxxiv + 426pp. 9 x 12.
                                                                          22503-8 Paperbound $5.00

VISUAL ILLUSIONS: THEIR CAUSES, CHARACTERISTICS, AND APPLICATIONS, Matthew Luckiesh. Thorough description and discussion of optical illusion, geometric and perspective, particularly; size and shape distortions, illusions of color, of motion; natural illusions; use of illusion in art and magic, industry, etc. Most useful today with op art, also for classical art. Scores of effects illustrated. Introduction by William H. Ittleson. 100 illustrations. xxi + 252pp.
21530-X Paperbound $2.00

A HANDBOOK OF ANATOMY FOR ART STUDENTS, Arthur Thomson. Thorough, virtually exhaustive coverage of skeletal structure, musculature, etc. Full text, supplemented by anatomical diagrams and drawings and by photographs of undraped figures. Unique in its comparison of male and female forms, pointing out differences of contour, texture, form. 211 figures, 40 drawings, 86 photographs. xx + 459pp. 5⅜ x 8⅜.
21163-0 Paperbound $3.50

150 MASTERPIECES OF DRAWING, Selected by Anthony Toney. Full page reproductions of drawings from the early 16th to the end of the 18th century, all beautifully reproduced: Rembrandt, Michelangelo, Dürer, Fragonard, Urs, Graf, Wouwerman, many others. First-rate browsing book, model book for artists. xviii + 150pp. 8⅜ x 11¼.
21032-4 Paperbound $2.50

THE LATER WORK OF AUBREY BEARDSLEY, Aubrey Beardsley. Exotic, erotic, ironic masterpieces in full maturity: Comedy Ballet, Venus and Tannhauser, Pierrot, Lysistrata, Rape of the Lock, Savoy material, Ali Baba, Volpone, etc. This material revolutionized the art world, and is still powerful, fresh, brilliant. With *The Early Work*, all Beardsley's finest work. 174 plates, 2 in color. xiv + 176pp. 8⅛ x 11.
21817-1 Paperbound $3.75

DRAWINGS OF REMBRANDT, Rembrandt van Rijn. Complete reproduction of fabulously rare edition by Lippmann and Hofstede de Groot, completely reedited, updated, improved by Prof. Seymour Slive, Fogg Museum. Portraits, Biblical sketches, landscapes, Oriental types, nudes, episodes from classical mythology—All Rembrandt's fertile genius. Also selection of drawings by his pupils and followers. "Stunning volumes," *Saturday Review*. 550 illustrations. lxxviii + 552pp. 9⅛ x 12¼.
21485-0, 21486-9 Two volumes, Paperbound $10.00

THE DISASTERS OF WAR, Francisco Goya. One of the masterpieces of Western civilization—83 etchings that record Goya's shattering, bitter reaction to the Napoleonic war that swept through Spain after the insurrection of 1808 and to war in general. Reprint of the first edition, with three additional plates from Boston's Museum of Fine Arts. All plates facsimile size. Introduction by Philip Hofer, Fogg Museum. v + 97pp. 9⅜ x 8¼.
21872-4 Paperbound $2.50

GRAPHIC WORKS OF ODILON REDON. Largest collection of Redon's graphic works ever assembled: 172 lithographs, 28 etchings and engravings, 9 drawings. These include some of his most famous works. All the plates from *Odilon Redon: oeuvre graphique complet,* plus additional plates. New introduction and caption translations by Alfred Werner. 209 illustrations. xxvii + 209pp. 9⅛ x 12¼.
21966-8 Paperbound $4.50

THE RED FAIRY BOOK, Andrew Lang. Lang's color fairy books have long been children's favorites. This volume includes Rapunzel, Jack and the Bean-stalk and 35 other stories, familiar and unfamiliar. 4 plates, 93 illustrations x + 367pp.
21673-X Paperbound $2.50

THE BLUE FAIRY BOOK, Andrew Lang. Lang's tales come from all countries and all times. Here are 37 tales from Grimm, the Arabian Nights, Greek Mythology, and other fascinating sources. 8 plates, 130 illustrations. xi + 390pp.
21437-0 Paperbound $2.75

HOUSEHOLD STORIES BY THE BROTHERS GRIMM. Classic English-language edition of the well-known tales — Rumpelstiltskin, Snow White, Hansel and Gretel, The Twelve Brothers, Faithful John, Rapunzel, Tom Thumb (52 stories in all). Translated into simple, straightforward English by Lucy Crane. Ornamented with head-pieces, vignettes, elaborate decorative initials and a dozen full-page illustrations by Walter Crane. x + 269pp.
21080-4 Paperbound **$2.00**

THE MERRY ADVENTURES OF ROBIN HOOD, Howard Pyle. The finest modern versions of the traditional ballads and tales about the great English outlaw. Howard Pyle's complete prose version, with every word, every illustration of the first edition. Do not confuse this facsimile of the original (1883) with modern editions that change text or illustrations. 23 plates plus many page decorations. xxii + 296pp.
22043-5 Paperbound $2.75

THE STORY OF KING ARTHUR AND HIS KNIGHTS, Howard Pyle. The finest children's version of the life of King Arthur; brilliantly retold by Pyle, with 48 of his most imaginative illustrations. xviii + 313pp. 6⅛ x 9¼.
21445-1 Paperbound $2.50

THE WONDERFUL WIZARD OF OZ, L. Frank Baum. America's finest children's book in facsimile of first edition with all Denslow illustrations in full color. The edition a child should have. Introduction by Martin Gardner. 23 color plates, scores of drawings. iv + 267pp.
20691-2 Paperbound $3.50

THE MARVELOUS LAND OF OZ, L. Frank Baum. The second Oz book, every bit as imaginative as the Wizard. The hero is a boy named Tip, but the Scarecrow and the Tin Woodman are back, as is the Oz magic. 16 color plates, 120 drawings by John R. Neill. 287pp.
20692-0 Paperbound $2.50

THE MAGICAL MONARCH OF MO, L. Frank Baum. Remarkable adventures in a land even stranger than Oz. The best of Baum's books not in the Oz series. 15 color plates and dozens of drawings by Frank Verbeck. xviii + 237pp.
21892-9 Paperbound $2.25

THE BAD CHILD'S BOOK OF BEASTS, MORE BEASTS FOR WORSE CHILDREN, A MORAL ALPHABET, Hilaire Belloc. Three complete humor classics in one volume. Be kind to the frog, and do not call him names . . . and 28 other whimsical animals. Familiar favorites and some not so well known. Illustrated by Basil Blackwell. 156pp.
(USO) 20749-8 Paperbound $1.50

CATALOGUE OF DOVER BOOKS

EAST O' THE SUN AND WEST O' THE MOON, George W. Dasent. Considered the best of all translations of these Norwegian folk tales, this collection has been enjoyed by generations of children (and folklorists too). Includes True and Untrue, Why the Sea is Salt, East O' the Sun and West O' the Moon, Why the Bear is Stumpy-Tailed, Boots and the Troll, The Cock and the Hen, Rich Peter the Pedlar, and 52 more. The only edition with all 59 tales. 77 illustrations by Erik Werenskiold and Theodor Kittelsen. xv + 418pp. 22521-6 Paperbound $3.50

GOOPS AND HOW TO BE THEM, Gelett Burgess. Classic of tongue-in-cheek humor, masquerading as etiquette book. 87 verses, twice as many cartoons, show mischievous Goops as they demonstrate to children virtues of table manners, neatness, courtesy, etc. Favorite for generations. viii + 88pp. 6½ x 9¼.
22233-0 Paperbound $1.50

ALICE'S ADVENTURES UNDER GROUND, Lewis Carroll. The first version, quite different from the final Alice in Wonderland, printed out by Carroll himself with his own illustrations. Complete facsimile of the "million dollar" manuscript Carroll gave to Alice Liddell in 1864. Introduction by Martin Gardner. viii + 96pp. Title and dedication pages in color. 21482-6 Paperbound $1.25

THE BROWNIES, THEIR BOOK, Palmer Cox. Small as mice, cunning as foxes, exuberant and full of mischief, the Brownies go to the zoo, toy shop, seashore, circus, etc., in 24 verse adventures and 266 illustrations. Long a favorite, since their first appearance in St. Nicholas Magazine. xi + 144pp. 6⅝ x 9¼.
21265-3 Paperbound $1.75

SONGS OF CHILDHOOD, Walter De La Mare. Published (under the pseudonym Walter Ramal) when De La Mare was only 29, this charming collection has long been a favorite children's book. A facsimile of the first edition in paper, the 47 poems capture the simplicity of the nursery rhyme and the ballad, including such lyrics as I Met Eve, Tartary, The Silver Penny. vii + 106pp. (USO) 21972-0 Paperbound $1.25

THE COMPLETE NONSENSE OF EDWARD LEAR, Edward Lear. The finest 19th-century humorist-cartoonist in full: all nonsense limericks, zany alphabets, Owl and Pussycat, songs, nonsense botany, and more than 500 illustrations by Lear himself. Edited by Holbrook Jackson. xxix + 287pp. (USO) 20167-8 Paperbound $2.00

BILLY WHISKERS: THE AUTOBIOGRAPHY OF A GOAT, Frances Trego Montgomery. A favorite of children since the early 20th century, here are the escapades of that rambunctious, irresistible and mischievous goat—Billy Whiskers. Much in the spirit of Peck's Bad Boy, this is a book that children never tire of reading or hearing. All the original familiar illustrations by W. H. Fry are included: 6 color plates, 18 black and white drawings. 159pp. 22345-0 Paperbound $2.00

MOTHER GOOSE MELODIES. Faithful republication of the fabulously rare Munroe and Francis "copyright 1833" Boston edition—the most important Mother Goose collection, usually referred to as the "original." Familiar rhymes plus many rare ones, with wonderful old woodcut illustrations. Edited by E. F. Bleiler. 128pp. 4½ x 6⅜. 22577-1 Paperbound $1.00

MATHEMATICAL PUZZLES FOR BEGINNERS AND ENTHUSIASTS, Geoffrey Mott-Smith. 189 puzzles from easy to difficult—involving arithmetic, logic, algebra, properties of digits, probability, etc.—for enjoyment and mental stimulus. Explanation of mathematical principles behind the puzzles. 135 illustrations. viii + 248pp.
20198-8 Paperbound $2.00

PAPER FOLDING FOR BEGINNERS, William D. Murray and Francis J. Rigney. Easiest book on the market, clearest instructions on making interesting, beautiful origami. Sail boats, cups, roosters, frogs that move legs, bonbon boxes, standing birds, etc. 40 projects; more than 275 diagrams and photographs. 94pp.
20713-7 Paperbound $1.00

TRICKS AND GAMES ON THE POOL TABLE, Fred Herrmann. 79 tricks and games— some solitaires, some for two or more players, some competitive games—to entertain you between formal games. Mystifying shots and throws, unusual caroms, tricks involving such props as cork, coins, a hat, etc. Formerly *Fun on the Pool Table.* 77 figures. 95pp.
21814-7 Paperbound $1.25

HAND SHADOWS TO BE THROWN UPON THE WALL: A SERIES OF NOVEL AND AMUSING FIGURES FORMED BY THE HAND, Henry Bursill. Delightful picturebook from great-grandfather's day shows how to make 18 different hand shadows: a bird that flies, duck that quacks, dog that wags his tail, camel, goose, deer, boy, turtle, etc. Only book of its sort. vi + 33pp. 6½ x 9¼. 21779-5 Paperbound $1.00

WHITTLING AND WOODCARVING, E. J. Tangerman. 18th printing of best book on market. "If you can cut a potato you can carve" toys and puzzles, chains, chessmen, caricatures, masks, frames, woodcut blocks, surface patterns, much more. Information on tools, woods, techniques. Also goes into serious wood sculpture from Middle Ages to present, East and West. 464 photos, figures. x + 293pp.
20965-2 Paperbound $2.50

HISTORY OF PHILOSOPHY, Julián Marias. Possibly the clearest, most easily followed, best planned, most useful one-volume history of philosophy on the market; neither skimpy nor overfull. Full details on system of every major philosopher and dozens of less important thinkers from pre-Socratics up to Existentialism and later. Strong on many European figures usually omitted. Has gone through dozens of editions in Europe. 1966 edition, translated by Stanley Appelbaum and Clarence Strowbridge. xviii + 505pp. 21739-6 Paperbound $3.50

YOGA: A SCIENTIFIC EVALUATION, Kovoor T. Behanan. Scientific but non-technical study of physiological results of yoga exercises; done under auspices of Yale U. Relations to Indian thought, to psychoanalysis, etc. 16 photos. xxiii + 270pp.
20505-3 Paperbound $2.50

Prices subject to change without notice.
Available at your book dealer or write for free catalogue to Dept. GI, Dover Publications, Inc., 180 Varick St., N. Y., N. Y. 10014. Dover publishes more than 150 books each year on science, elementary and advanced mathematics, biology, music, art, literary history, social sciences and other areas.